The PayPal Official Insider Guide to
SOCIAL MEDIA

Make money through viral marketing

Brian Proffitt

PayPal™ / Press

The PayPal Official Insider Guide to Social Media
Brian Proffitt

This PayPal Press book is published by Peachpit.
For information on PayPal Press books, contact:

Peachpit
1249 Eighth Street
Berkeley, CA 94710
510/524-2178
510/524-2221 (fax)

Find us on the Web at: www.peachpit.com
To report errors, please send a note to errata@peachpit.com

Copyright © 2012 by Brian Proffitt

Project Editor: Michael J. Nolan
Development Editor: Marta Justak
PayPal Press Managing Editor: Matthew T. Jones
Production Editor: David Van Ness
Copyeditor: Marta Justak
Proofreader: Jan Seymour
Indexer: Rebecca Plunkett
Cover and Interior Designer: Charlene Charles-Will
Compositor: Myrna Vladic

ISBN 13:   978-0-321-80480-8
ISBN 10:   0-321-80480-5

9 8 7 6 5 4 3 2 1

Printed and bound in the United States of America

For Jhett
Live long and fight on

Acknowledgments

AUTHOR'S ACKNOWLEDGEMENTS

My wife likes to say that I'm the kind of geek that you can take to parties. Which, I suppose, means that I'm just social enough that I can talk to people without their eyes glazing over in a wash of conversation about mobile phone platforms, Linux kernel headers, and the intricacies of display drivers.

I credit her, along with three fabulous daughters, for keeping my nerd aura down to a minimum, by showing me that there's more to life than circuit boards. Knowing that lets me broaden my horizons and enables me to write books like this.

The teams at PayPal Press and Peachpit get a big helping of thanks for providing their time and insights into producing this book.

Finally, my editor Marta Justak gets my highest praise for her professionalism and expertise. She makes my words better, and makes book writing more of a joy than a chore.

PAYPAL PRESS ACKNOWLEDGEMENTS

We applaud PayPal Product Managers Tanya Urschel and Keith Koenig, whose great subject-matter expertise was matched only by their dedication; Janet Ball, our Marketing Manager, whose thorough knowledge of social media provided invaluable research; PayPal Press Managing Editor Matt Jones, whose expert content strategy ensured top editorial quality; Production Editors Raji Nayak and Karen Richards, whose diligent teamwork mastered our ambitious schedule; and John Heisch, our Illustrator, whose astute artwork enhanced the value of this book.

PayPal Press would also like to thank the following team members for their creative talents and constructive contributions: Janet Isadore, David Hershfield, Sarah Brody, Jonah Otis, Smitha Koppuzha, Cynthia Robinson, Cynthia Maller, Anjali Desai, Eunice Louie, J.B. Coutinho, Jamie Patricio, Sudha Jamthe, and Perrine Crampton.

Foreword

Shopping has always been an inherently social endeavor—whether it's serendipitously finding a great deal at a local boutique or going on a mission with a close friend to find the perfect accessory for a big event. Human interactions and shared experiences are a vital part of the appeal of shopping. And it's no surprise that today these same experiences have moved online, thanks in part to the rise of social media.

The explosion of consumer interest and participation in social networks has naturally and quickly moved into social commerce. Transacting within social networks is predicted to rise from $5 billion in 2011 to $30 billion by 2015. What's more, analysts predict that by 2015, companies will generate 50 percent of Web sales via their social presence and mobile applications.

PayPal thrives at the heart of this emerging social commerce era. Our mission is to define the future of shopping and paying, allowing anyone to pay anytime and anywhere. And we're doing this by making *paying* more social. Already, you can find PayPal in numerous group buying and group gifting apps, powering "social shopping malls" on the most popular social networks, and on millions of mobile devices that share shopping experiences, local deals, and more.

Ever-more retailers are experimenting with new ways to utilize social media to connect with customers and drive sales. At PayPal, our core social media tenets include listening, participating, and adding value. After all, at its core, social media is about building deeper connections with people. We're committed to helping our customers seize the social commerce opportunity. This area will see significant innovation in the coming years, and PayPal will be a driving force.

—Amanda Pires
Senior Director of Global Communications
PayPal

Contents at a Glance

Contents

Part 4 MONETIZING SOCIAL MEDIA WITH PAYPAL

Introduction

"Social media" is not new. Human community and conversation have been hallmarks of civilization for thousands of years.

Throughout history, when differing groups (families, tribes, or other units) of people would meet, shared commerce would often be the basis of their communication. What did one group have that the other needed? What would be accepted for trade?

This is how social communication has worked over time among many cultures. Some cultures may not have liked each other, but they would often find a way to talk and trade, despite their differences. In fact, trade often became the reason for communication, as trading tribes became communities that ultimately expanded and grew into our present society.

In Western cultures today, however, the need for face-to-face communication has faded somewhat. The advent of the telephone and the automobile redefined the nature of communities. But while modern ways may have changed the structure of the community, we have not done away with our need to be together. After all, we still love to socialize.

We see this now in the popularity of new social media, as technology enables us to connect to each other and form social groups not based on material survival alone but on other, more personalized interests. Today's technologies allow communities to form as "instant" networks of people who discover they have much in common to share. Parents exchange child-rearing tips through like-minded community websites. Doctors conduct combined research—in real time—with peers linked at other labs. Teachers run virtual classrooms with children across the globe.

We are still trading—only now the common currency is information.

For PayPal, which helps facilitate faster, easier, safer commerce online, social media is yet another opportunity to assist its customers. Organizations today have exciting new ways to share profitable opportunities through social media and viral marketing. PayPal recognizes this, and helps serve merchants who are eager to fully utilize social media to grow their businesses.

In *The PayPal Official Insider Guide to Social Media*, you will learn the following:

- How to navigate the social media landscape

- The best way to plan and implement a social media branding strategy

- How to create content for social media networks

- How PayPal tools provide an effective ecommerce solution that works with your social media strategy

This book will help retailers understand the basics of social media and how to engage and prosper in conversations with their customers.

Part 1

UNDERSTANDING PAYPAL FOR SOCIAL MEDIA

1

Learning How PayPal Works

Wherever there are people, there has always been a way to get *stuff*.

From the earliest days of hanging around the savannah, trying to get something to eat and avoid being eaten, people have always desired stuff and needed a way to get said stuff. Sometimes, alas, people would resort to hitting people with large sticks to get stuff, but for the most part, it was a lot easier to just trade other stuff people didn't need for the stuff that they wanted.

Eventually, the idea of transactions (aka "stuff") became a bit more formalized, and now we conduct transactions whenever and wherever people are gathered—in forests, on airplanes, under the ocean, and on the Internet. And where transactions occur on the Internet, most often you'll find PayPal.

The PayPal Tool

Before we learn how PayPal aligns with social media and the various tools for social media that are out there, it's important to have an understanding of the basics of PayPal.

PayPal is often referred to as an *online payment tool*, but in reality that description is far off the mark. What PayPal offers its users is a safer and more secure way to conduct transactions on the Web. If your customers use PayPal to conduct transactions, what they get is peace of mind knowing their transactions are secure from prying eyes.

Transaction 101

Let's say, for example, that you are the customer, visiting a website that uses the PayPal service to handle transactions. You've found the

Figure 1.1
A typical PayPal transaction sequence.

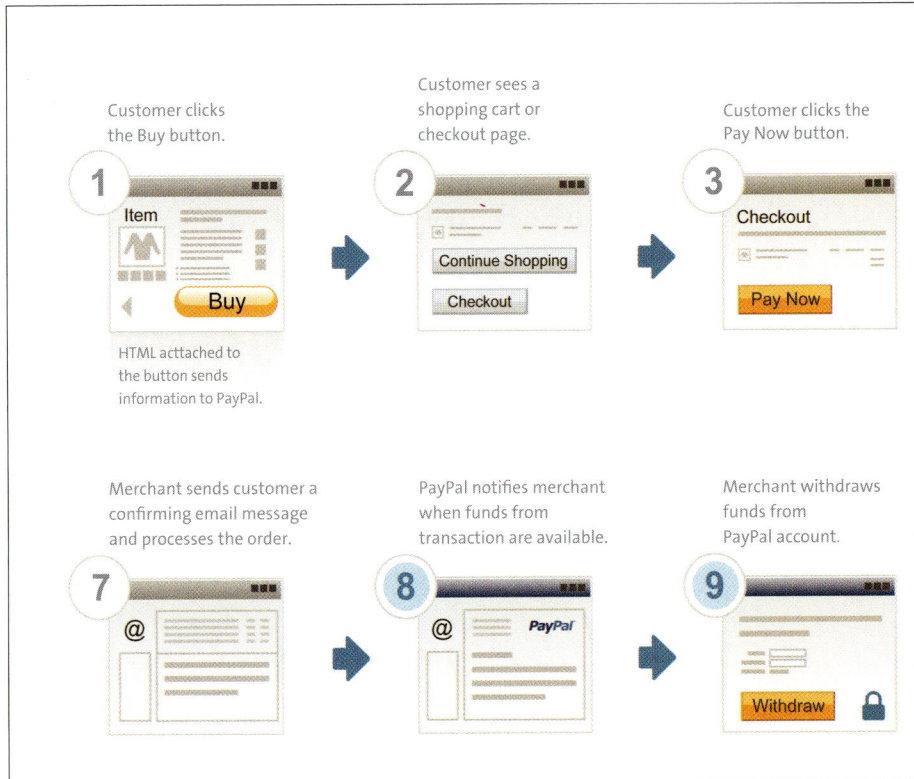

Customer clicks the Buy button.

1

Item

Buy

HTML acttached to the button sends information to PayPal.

Customer sees a shopping cart or checkout page.

2

Continue Shopping

Checkout

Customer clicks the Pay Now button.

3

Checkout

Pay Now

Merchant sends customer a confirming email message and processes the order.

7

@

PayPal notifies merchant when funds from transaction are available.

8

@   *PayPal*

Merchant withdraws funds from PayPal account.

9

Withdraw

perfect-sized print of Van Gogh's *Starry Night* for your den, and you want to order it now, while supplies last. **Figure 1.1** illustrates the steps your transaction will take.

The whole transaction starts when you find that print you're looking for on Masterpieces-R-Us.com (obviously, a fictitious site). You click on the Van Gogh print on its product page and then click the Buy button.

Right here, PayPal may already be in action. If the website uses only PayPal for transaction handling, and you have followed PayPal's instructions and inserted the correct HTML code onto the Buy button, then PayPal will be sent a command and will take over the remainder of the transaction process. If there are other payment options, PayPal will receive the information and take over the process later (in Step 4). You can, if you want, shop for other stuff, but for this example, let's say you're set to go.

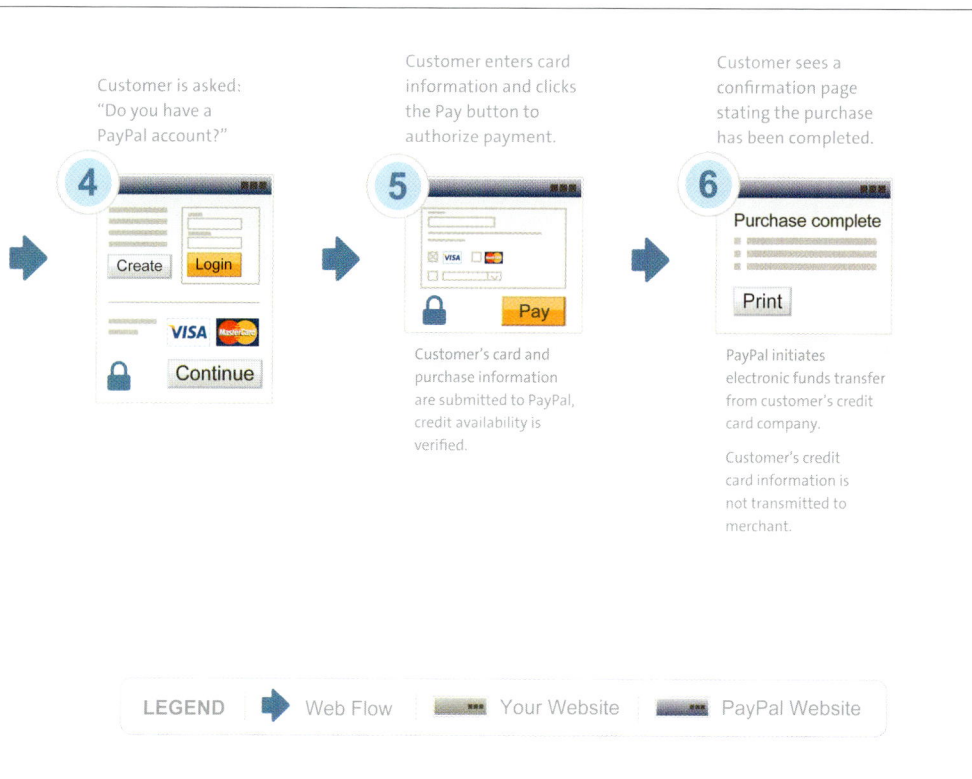

Customer is asked: "Do you have a PayPal account?"

Customer enters card information and clicks the Pay button to authorize payment.

Customer sees a confirmation page stating the purchase has been completed.

4 Create | Login | VISA MasterCard | Continue

5 VISA | Pay

6 Purchase complete | Print

Customer's card and purchase information are submitted to PayPal, credit availability is verified.

PayPal initiates electronic funds transfer from customer's credit card company.

Customer's credit card information is not transmitted to merchant.

LEGEND — Web Flow — Your Website — PayPal Website

The following steps will walk you through the actions illustrated in Figure 1.1.

1. Click the Buy button. The shopping cart or checkout page will open.

2. Here, things can vary as far as the exact step because the merchant may rely a lot on PayPal for the checkout process, or very little. So you might see a checkout page at the merchant's site itself, or one that appears to be the merchant website but is actually hosted and managed by PayPal. A third possibility will be a page that's clearly hosted by PayPal but carries the merchant's logo.

   However this step appears to the customer, you will see your product listed and other necessary information such as price, shipping and handling charges, and applicable sales tax.

3. If it all looks in order, click the Buy Now button, which will open the payment page.

4. Again, this is where things will diverge a bit. If PayPal is the only payment option, you will see a PayPal page and have the opportunity to log in or sign up for a new account. If PayPal is one payment option among many, you will have an extra step of choosing PayPal first. For this example, let's presume you selected PayPal as the payment option. *Now* information about the purchase is sent to PayPal, since PayPal is now taking over the transaction.

NOTE: If you have a user account already, you can just log in with your user name and password, and all of the rest of your personal information—address, phone number, and payment info—are pulled from PayPal's records about you and entered into the payment form.

5. If you don't have a PayPal account, this is the point where you can create one for yourself. (All of your transaction information will be saved until you get back to the transaction after registering for PayPal's service.) Or you don't need to create an account at all. On the PayPal payment page, just enter all of your personal information and credit card information into the form. Click Pay to begin the payment authorization process.

As soon as you click Pay, your credit card information is sent to PayPal, which contacts either your credit card's issuing bank or your personal bank if you've chosen to use funds from a bank account. Assuming that your credit card or bank account can afford the purchase, the appropriate bank will authorize the transaction, and the sale will be charged. However, the sale is *not* charged to the merchant; it's charged to PayPal. (This is important for security reasons that will be mentioned later.)

NOTE: All PayPal transactions take place on Web pages that utilize Secure Sockets Layer (SSL) encryption. SSL encryption protects the customer's personal data, because even if the information is intercepted, it cannot be read.

6. On your screen, you will see a PayPal confirmation page in your browser which informs you that your transaction has been completed. Simultaneously, the merchant will also be notified by PayPal of the purchase, usually with an email message that includes information about the purchased item and your shipping information. But that's not all. At the same time, an electronic funds transfer (EFT) is initiated from your bank or the credit card bank to PayPal. This is started now because EFTs can take a while to process.

   It's important to note that at no time in the process has the retailer actually seen any of your financial information. The merchant knows your name and address by now, for shipping purposes, but that's it. This keeps the sensitive data held between you and PayPal private and confidential.

7. Even though the retailer hasn't received any funds from PayPal yet, the retailer will usually start processing the order at this point. The product is picked off the warehouse shelf, boxed, and labeled for shipment. Digital products, such as music or software files, can be made ready for immediate download. The merchant may even send you a note letting you know that the transaction is ticking right along.

8. Meanwhile, PayPal has been waiting for that EFT to be completed and for funds from your bank or credit card to be dropped into their account. Once your money arrives, PayPal will immediately turn around and credit the retailer's PayPal account with the money from the transaction—minus (and this is important) applicable fees. At the same time, the retailer will be notified that the funds are in the retailer's account.

9. The retailer can, when it's convenient, withdraw the funds from the PayPal account.

Meanwhile, you have the print to hang in your den, and all is well.

These are the basic steps of the transaction: PayPal receives your purchase information, transmits the order to the merchant, receives payment from your source account (PayPal balance, bank, or credit card), and then PayPal credits the retailer's account, taking its fees out along the way.

Did You Say Fees?

NOTE: Fees are current as of September 2011, but are subject to change without notice.

Now that you've walked through the transaction process as a customer, you can put your retailer hat back on so we can talk about fees.

PayPal collects fees from the *merchant* in the transaction, not the buyer. The more payments you receive as a merchant each month, the less of a fee you'll have to pay per transaction.

PayPal INSIDER

Our Business Model

PayPal is in business to serve our customers, and also to make a profit for our stakeholders.

You might be surprised to learn that the fees we collect from merchants don't always generate a lot of profit. That's because we have to pay fees of our own to the credit card companies to use their processing networks when credit cards are used. These processing costs are very close to the fees that we charge our merchants.

In other words, we try to keep our fees as low as possible.

Instead, we make most of our profits from interest on the money we handle. There's a lag between when we receive funds from the credit card companies and when those funds are withdrawn by our merchants. Even if it's only a day or two, during the time the funds reside in PayPal's corporate bank account, interest is earned on the money. Because we're handling a few million transactions a day, you can see how quickly the pennies add up. That's how we're able to offer such competitive card processing rates; we don't have to mark things up a lot.

Merchants pay PayPal a percentage of the total transaction amount (2.2 to 2.9%, depending on their monthly sales volume) plus $0.30 per transaction. PayPal pays you, the merchant, the total amount paid by the customer minus these transaction fees.

For example, let's say the Van Gogh print cost $50 plus $10 for shipping. (Let's leave out sales tax for a bit to make the example easier.) That's a total of $60 that PayPal receives from the customer for the art, but PayPal won't drop $60 into the retailer's PayPal account.

Assuming that the merchant does a low volume of business on a monthly basis, and has to pay the highest possible PayPal fee of 2.9%, then PayPal will hold $1.74 plus an additional 30-cent transaction fee. So that's $60 minus $1.74 minus $0.30, for a remainder of $57.96 that is deposited into the retailer's account. Put another way, the merchant pays $2.04 in fees to PayPal for this transaction.

This is a sliding scale (the more monthly sales, the lower the fee); for example, if the merchant clears over $100,000 in sales per month, then the transaction fee is lowered to only $1.44 ($1.14 plus the $0.30 flat fee). You'll read more on this later in the chapter.

Why Use PayPal?

Looking at the previous transaction steps, it's easy to see how PayPal is attractive to both the customers and merchants who use this service.

What Customers Get

Another of PayPal's big perks for customers is that at the bare minimum, it enables people to pay for items online with a credit card. (It can also enable direct transfer from a bank account, if customers so choose.) This may not seem like a big feature, but setting up an epayment system for a merchant is not as easy as you would think. There would be a lot fewer merchants accepting credit card payments if PayPal weren't around to make things easier.

Regular PayPal users with accounts get even more out of the service. They can store their payment and shipment information within the PayPal system—information that will be transmitted to the merchant when the time comes. That's nice to have, so you don't have to enter your address in every time you buy something from a site.

PayPal customers can also set up a number of payment sources, such as a bank account or any one of a number of credit cards. Merchants can even configure department store cards, which will enable their customers to use the specific card for the matching store and thus gain more benefits from any loyalty program that their store might have.

TIP: PayPal acts as your electronic wallet, allowing you to change how you pay with each transaction—choose your bank account or any credit card stored in your account.

The way that PayPal handles transactions also affords quite a bit of security for the user. Since the merchant never actually sees the customer's financial information, that's one less set of eyes that might be tempted to abuse the information. PayPal also has a lot of experience with fraud attempts, and thus has a lot of savvy ways of preventing fraud, including buyer protection and PayPal mediator services. If something does go wrong with a purchase, PayPal's Purchase Program will step in and make things right for eligible transactions.

PayPal offers customers availability, convenience, and security.

What Merchants Get

Businesses get a lot of benefits from using PayPal, not the least of which is ease of use and competitive rates. But there are a lot of other benefits for merchants, too.

CREDIT CARD PAYMENTS

The capability to process credit cards is pretty much the minimum bar needed for anyone doing business online. But even with the proliferation of credit card ecommerce options, setting up an affordable credit card payment system is not as easy as it sounds. PayPal give merchants both: ease of use and affordability.

WHITE BOX ECOMMERCE SYSTEMS

Many website management tools, such as Joomla!, Drupal, and WordPress, all feature ecommerce modules that integrate well with your website. But what if you have a website built on HTML and ActiveX, or PHP, or some other scripting language? Integrating ecommerce tools and checkout pages into sites like this is often difficult and expensive work.

PayPal offers participating merchants a better option: a "white box" checkout system that can be customized to the look and feel of your site. White box is a term used to describe systems or products that can be rebranded to look and feel like another company's services. Shoppers will conclude their transactions on PayPal's site, but thanks to the nature of the customized checkout pages, they will have a seamless experience.

EASY SIGN-UP

Applying for a traditional merchant credit card account is, to put it mildly, hard. Not only do you have to give information about you, your business, and the names of your pet fish, but many credit card companies try to upsell you more features that they think you need, making the whole process an arduous chore—for which you have to pay the credit card company in the end. And after all that, you may end up paying a rate that's more than you anticipated.

PayPal's registration to create a basic business account is pretty much a one-page deal, with common-sense questions that don't leave you feeling like you've given a pint of blood. And the fees are straightforward: if you do X amount of business a month, you will pay X fees, just as simple as that. PayPal is also accommodating to smaller businesses that might not otherwise qualify for a merchant credit card account.

NOTE: If you want to add Website Payments Pro service to your account, you do need to apply and be vetted, which can require additional information and time. The Website Payments Pro service provides a fully functional merchant checkout and payment gateway, as detailed at www.paypal.com/webapps/mpp/website-payments-pro.

SECURITY

The way that PayPal handles transactions not only gives customers more security, but it also affords businesses additional security. If a bad transaction goes through PayPal, such as an uncovered purchase, the merchant will likely never see it, since PayPal handles the fund confirmation process.

If a fraudulent transaction does go through, PayPal's seller protection program can step in and facilitate a solution for eligible transactions.

PCI COMPLIANCE

The Payment Card Industry Data Security Standard, or PCI DSS, is a set of requirements designed to make sure that any merchant or bank is handling credit card transactions in a secure environment.

Any business with a merchant credit card account has to be PCI DSS-compliant, which includes completing an annual self-assessment and quarterly system scans. That's your time and your money.

PayPal solutions like Website Payments Standard, which enables Payment buttons on products on your site, or Express Checkout, which creates a fast checkout process for PayPal users, however, don't impose such a compliance requirement on you as the merchant, because merchants never see the customer's information, remember? If there is no credit card data, there's no need for PCI DSS compliance. That's PayPal's concern, and you get the convenience of PayPal handling this compliance issue on your behalf.

Of course, if you do handle your own credit card data and use PayPal as a separate payment option, you'll still have to maintain your own PCI DSS compliance.

LOWER COSTS

With the increased security and reduced administrative overhead for transactions, PayPal is very likely going to be less expensive than using credit card processing. With less fraud, fewer chargebacks and customer complaints on transactions, PayPal helps free your staff to work on more important things, like generating more revenue.

BETTER REPUTATION

PayPal has been around long enough to establish a fairly strong reputation as a more secure way to pay for goods, services, and even donations to charities. With PayPal on your site, you can reassure your customers that you're not some fly-by-night website that's going to take their money and run.

GO GLOBAL

Want to send your stuff overseas? If you can manage international shipping, then there's no other barrier for your business to work with international customers. PayPal can easily handle currency conversion and applicable fees of an international transaction, thus increasing your sales. This is a brilliant advantage to have, since a lot of social media conversations will happen on an international level and may encourage international sales.

CATCH THE ONLINE WAVE

So not only can PayPal's reputation help you get more sales, but there's also evidence that PayPal users are more inclined to buy something from your site if you have PayPal, and not just because of PayPal's reputation. In fact, PayPal users tend to shop more frequently and spend more money online than do non-PayPal users, so you should reap those benefits right away.

How great is the benefit that we're talking about here?

A 2010 PayPal survey of 805 PayPal merchants found that small- to medium-sized businesses that offered PayPal Express Checkout in addition to traditional credit card payments registered an 18 percent average increase in sales after implementing PayPal.

Plus, over 80 percent of those merchants surveyed reported some sort of sales increase from the PayPal option, and the increase typically started within two months of implementation. The increase was incremental and did not take away from existing credit card sales.

How Much Would You Pay?

That's a lot of benefit from PayPal, so what are the costs associated with the service, in detail?

⚠ **CAUTION:** It's important to note that PayPal's fees are based on the *total* money paid by the customer, not the actual price of the item. That means if you have a $50 item sold and there is a $10 shipping charge tacked on top of that, then PayPal bases its fees on the total $60 paid by the customer, not the $50 price of the item.

As mentioned, PayPal charges no fees to buyers; the merchant pays all of the fees for a given transaction. With every transaction, there are two fees charged: a sliding fee based on a percentage of the transaction amount (that percentage being based on the amount of business you do per month) and a flat per-transaction fee.

As of September 2011, PayPal's percentage transaction fees ranged from 2.2 to 2.9%, depending on your company's monthly sales volume. Add a flat $0.30 fee per transaction, and you have the total fee.

PayPal INSIDER

🏠 Simplifying the Fees You Pay

PayPal's fees are fairly simple. Depending on your monthly sales volume, we charge between 2.2 and 2.9% of the total transaction, plus $0.30 per transaction. It doesn't matter what payment method the customer uses, or who the customer is: your fees are the same.

That's not the case with traditional merchant credit card processing services. Fee structures can be very complex. If consumers use special "vanity" cards, for example, you (the merchant) pay a higher fee without the consumer's knowledge. There are many variables, which makes planning difficult and reporting cumbersome.

At PayPal, we prefer to take that completely out of the equation for our merchant customers. We charge you the same rate no matter which card a customer is using. The 2.9% (or lower) rate applies to all purchases.

This is important to keep in mind when comparing rates between PayPal and other services. In addition to setup fees, fixed monthly fees, and terminal/software fees, you should compare the transaction fees charged, and whether they are variable.

Table 1.1 presents PayPal's U.S. fee schedule as of September 2011 (subject to change):

Table 1.1 PayPal's U.S. Merchant Fees

Monthly Sales	Transaction Fee
$0–$3,000.00	2.9% + $0.30
$3,000.01–$10,000.00	2.5% + $0.30
$10,000.01–$100,000.00	2.2% + $0.30

Other fees may apply, such as the monthly fees for Website Payments Pro, Virtual Terminal, or cross-border fees.

CAUTION: When comparing PayPal fees with traditional merchant credit card processors, be sure to include all the fees charged, such as the fees for renting a terminal, leasing processing software, and so on.

Learn More

As you may have been able to tell, there are a lot more services that PayPal offers than just the basic transactions mentioned here. Some of those additional services will be the focus of this book, particularly the tools that integrate with social media and social strategies.

But to learn more about PayPal's business services fast, surf to PayPal's website at www.paypal.com and the other books in the *PayPal Official Insider Guide* series. Click the Business tab to see a page similar to the one shown in **Figure 1.2** on the following page, and explore the site to discover more tools to help your business grow.

Figure 1.2

Look online to learn more about PayPal's business services.

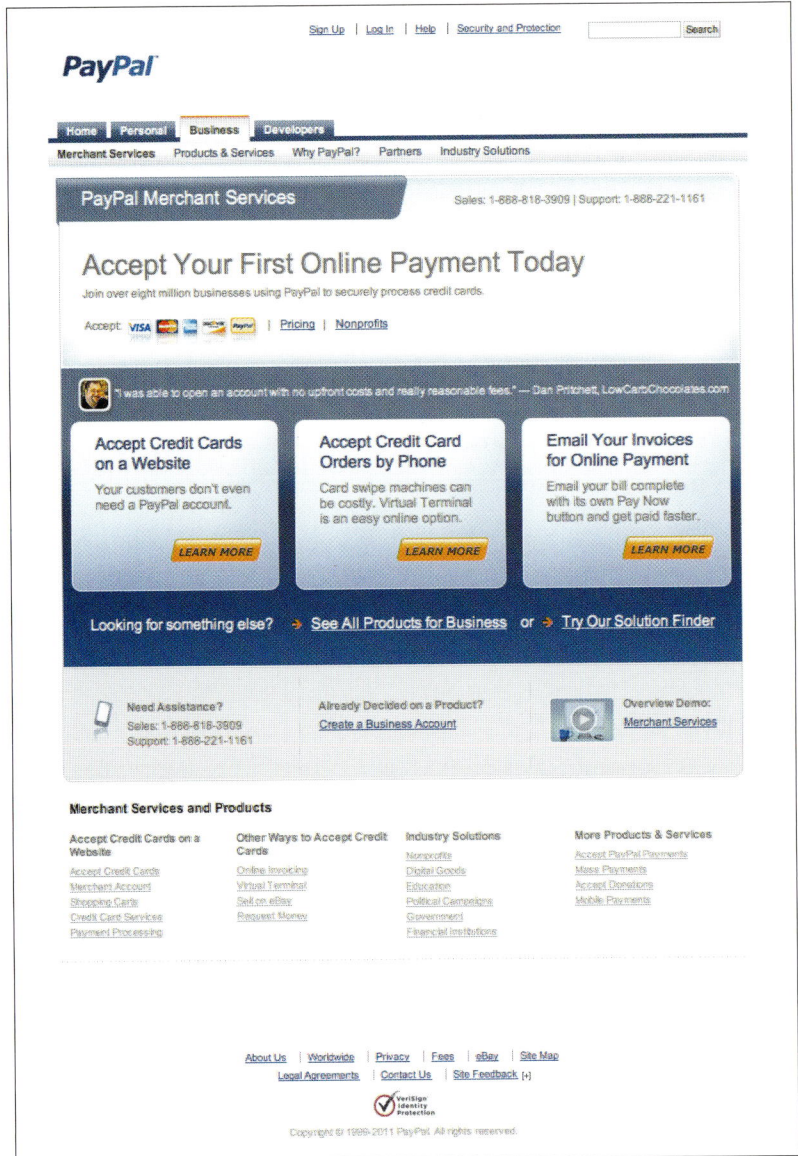

The PayPal website also features a help system designed for both consumers and merchants. Click the Help link on any page to find an extensive list of support topics, or use the Search field to narrow your search. There is even a PayPal Community Support Forum, where you can get questions answered from fellow PayPal users.

The Last Word

PayPal is one of the world's largest online payment services, and it has become a recognized name in Internet commerce as a safe and affordable way to conduct business on the Internet. Businesses and customers alike will appreciate the simplicity of transactions and of setting up ecommerce tools on a merchant website.

This ease of use also translates well into how you can integrate PayPal with social media strategies for your business.

In Chapter 2, "Charting the Social Commerce Landscape," we'll begin to examine how your organization can get started on entering the conversations that define the world of social media.

2

Charting the Social Commerce Landscape

We, as human beings, like to talk. Perhaps not to each other, perhaps not as often as we would like, or perhaps even too often, but we can't ignore that we were born to talk. Or write. Or sign. Even before we figured out the whole thing with stuff, we figured out ways to get our thoughts across to one another.

When we figured out a way to connect ourselves to each other via nearly every electronic device on the planet, we figured out how to communicate in that medium as well. Email, chat sessions, text messages, Tweets, and the like…as time went by, our Internet conversations mirrored those we had in the large world around us. We even came up with a catchy name: social media.

Social media is a story of technology, but more importantly, it's a story of human existence.

Social Business

All business, really, is social. How could it be otherwise? Exchanging goods and services is little different than exchanging ideas and thoughts. There's just a little more structure to it: certain rules of the road need to be followed, such as paying someone fairly after receiving the goods, or making sure you actually give people what they paid for.

Those rules are rather rigid and less free flowing than an actual conversation because there are things of value involved, and both sides want things to be fair. That is a big part of why we haven't seen a lot of transaction tools integrated into social media platforms yet; it's not easy implementing a transaction system that is safe and secure within an environment that was not designed for ecommerce. Social networks are great at conversations, but not so great (yet) at commerce.

Plus, let's face it, a lot of us don't want commerce to interject itself in our conversations. It would be awkward if we were talking with someone and just randomly started chatting about that great new shampoo we got yesterday. Life is not a commercial.

But there are times when conversation does flow in a direction where commerce can be brought up. How many times have we heard a friend complain about a given product or service, and we then recommended that she try something better? At that point, wouldn't it be nice to send her a link to the item, or better yet, a link to actually buy the product?

And it's not always going to be commercial, either. A much more common way for commerce and conversation to interact will occur when there is a cause or fundraiser you want to mention or support. Here, it's even better to have the link to donate close at hand, because you can mention the charity or cause to friends and family who trust you, and they can jump right in and donate to that cause.

Social media platforms are all about open information distribution. This is problematic when it comes to your financial information. "Open" and "financial data" aren't two terms that mix particularly well. PayPal solves that by being the layer of "protection" for your financial information online, regardless of the medium in which the transaction is taking place: Web or social media.

This, then, is the intersection of social media and business, where conversation overlaps commerce.

Social Media SUCCESS STORY

C'est Cheese: Introduction

Mari Taylor is the owner of a small but successful fictional cheese and gourmet food store located in a mid-sized metropolitan city. The business has been growing steadily over the years, mostly through conventional advertising and word-of-mouth, because her business, C'est Cheese, is well regarded among gourmands in her city.

But the recent economic downturn, and the rise of more competition from online gourmet food sites, has gotten Mari concerned. Business growth has been flat of late, and there have been a few weeks here and there when business has been shrinking. Clearly, a new approach has to be tried.

Which has led Mari to start thinking about social media. With social media, Mari will be able to get the word out to existing and potential customers about C'est Cheese and hopefully bring them through the doors. Mari has a steady core of

devoted customers, and she knows that they will be helpful in spreading the word to other people, which makes social media a suitable method for her needs.

Mari's challenge, though, is that she is not very technologically savvy. She knows her way around the office computer, and she can navigate her store's website, but following the latest trends in technology is far less important to her than tracking the latest trends in goat cheese.

So now Mari is embarking on her own exploration of social media tools and platforms, in the hope of finding the right strategy for the growth of her own business.

Mari's story will continue in the next installment in Chapter 4, where she will discover which social media platforms her customers are using.

Transaction Tools

PayPal has been exploring appropriate uses of ecommerce tools for social media platforms since those platforms became an important part of the virtual landscape. But how these tools have been implemented reveals an important clue as to how PayPal is going about this.

The fact is, PayPal has been a stalwart presence on the ecommerce landscape for quite some time, but it is just now becoming integrated with social media.

It's something that's changing, but right now many of the PayPal commerce tools are centered on self-contained widgets that can be used in very specific, non-commercial instances.

To make sure that the immediate needs of consumers will be met, PayPal tools are being integrated into non-profit donation transactions first. Why? Well, there's still that whole problem of getting commerce integrated into the ongoing conversations that make up most social media platforms. Very few people want the equivalent of a sales pitch popping up in their own conversations.

And, more importantly, the consumer demand for having a transparent way of donating money to causes was a far greater initial need than having a way for acquiring commercial goods on a social media platform.

FundRazr

Collecting money for a cause, any cause, can sometimes be a frustrating process. First, you have to find people willing to give. Then they have to have money on them ("I don't have cash; can you take a check? Who do I make it out to?"), and if they want a receipt, you have to fill one out.

That's if everything goes smoothly. Sometimes you will reach out to potential donors and discover they don't understand who you are or what the cause is that you represent. Or they will pledge to donate but won't follow through.

One company, ConnectionPoint's FundRazr, has tapped directly into the security and processing power of PayPal to create an online tool that helps you raise money for your charitable organization or local cause.

FundRazr is available for use by both individual causes as well as non-profit organizations. It can also be used for individuals who raise money on behalf of an organization like a non-profit or school, as this helps route all funds directly to the organization so the individual doesn't have to manage the money and can just focus on promoting the cause.

ConnectionPoint's FundRazr app can be added to the wall of your Facebook account or that of your organization. FundRazr was one of the first apps that could actually run inside the news feed, making it more shareable and creating a ripple effect for social good.

Once on your Facebook wall, the FundRazr app enables your friends and family to click the Give button and give to your cause. Since they go through PayPal, their payments are more secure and instantaneous.

TIP: The FundRazr widget shows up in your News Feed, and you can update and repost it to your Facebook Wall as often as you like. Your friends can copy your FundRazr widget to their own Facebook pages and add messages of support to their own network. Each update to the widget can show up in your News Feed, adding a viral element to maximize the network effect. No matter how many times the widget is copied, all the funds donated are collected to the originating PayPal account.

PayPal INSIDER

Working with FundRazr

The idea for FundRazr was born when Daryl Hatton, the CEO of ConnectionPoint, saw the potential in using Facebook as a way to easily communicate with and raise money from the social network community that existed around a sports team. Since then, the FundRazr team has focused on building a system that makes it very easy for non-charity non-profit groups—such as sports teams, schools, clubs, and the like—to raise money using all the capabilities of social media: Facebook, Twitter, Google Plus, YouTube, websites, blogs, email, and so on.

As FundRazr developers rolled out the product, non-profits and political campaigns saw the benefit of the social media integration and pushed FundRazr to enhance the product for their needs as well.

The advantages of FundRazr are the deep integration it has with Facebook, the capability to install rich social media fundraising functionality into any website or blog with a couple of lines of HTML code, and the trust model FundRazr has developed that allows non-profit staff, school administrators and team managers to delegate fundraising responsibility to volunteers/parents/teachers/coaches and yet still maintain control of the money.

FundRazr helps you avoid a lot of fundraising and donation collection headaches, even as the simplicity of the collection method makes it easier for donors to give to your cause.

WhatGives!?

The donation app WhatGives!? also enables donors to click a single button and give money directly to a cause.

WhatGives!? has some different features, though. WhatGives!? widgets can be placed on Facebook, blogs, and Web pages.

WhatGives!? also has another benefit: the capability of being shared. As a fundraising organization, you can have supporters and friends of your organization copy the widget created by the WhatGives!? app and post that widget on their WhatGives!? walls. Not only does this get the collection tool for the charitable cause out there in front of more eyeballs, but all of the money collected goes right back into the central PayPal account, receiving funds for the cause.

One difference between the FundRazr and WhatGives!? widgets is the connectivity between the Facebook- and blog-based widgets. In FundRazr, if a widget reports a certain set of information, then that information will be reflected in all other instances of that widget, no matter where the widget is located.

WhatGives!? (and FundRazr, for that matter) helps avoid the often huge speed bump of donations coming in for an organization that are paid to an individual representative, who then has to collect the checks and cash and make sure they're all delivered properly to the main organization. It also helps get around the issue of checks made out to the supporter and not the organization proper.

WhatGives!? lets users send donations from multiple collection points into a central account, and being flexible in where the money can be posted makes it a great app for non-profits to use.

BigCanvass

In the U.S., it's nice to know that everyone can run for a political office. But although anyone can run, not everyone can afford it.

That's because of another truism in politics: campaigns cost money. Signs, buttons, and newspaper, radio, and TV ads—these all can rack up some serious costs.

Raising money for campaigns can be hard, thankless work sometimes. Not to mention that there are very strict campaign fundraising rules to which candidates must adhere. Anything, then, that can make the process easier would be welcome.

This is where BigCanvass comes in. A social giving app made by the same people who put together WhatGives!?, BigCanvass supports all of the same features of that app: postability on Facebook, blogs, Web pages, and copying of the widget by supporters onto their own Web pages.

BigCanvass adds more features specifically for campaigns, most notably detailed reports that many campaigns must have in order to comply with local and federal election laws. That contributor information is also a prime source for more supporter information down the road.

Electioneering is an expensive process, and BigCanvass is a handy tool to help mitigate that cost.

Social Commerce Tools

Thus far, the tools highlighted in this chapter are direct transaction tools that work with PayPal and a given social platform.

There are other tools out there that aren't transaction oriented; there's no PayPal connection waiting to be found here. These are apps and services that are designed to do one thing: get more customers in your door, and make sure those customers are satisfied.

ShopSocially

ShopSocially's Social Connect service lets shoppers on your commerce site become brand ambassadors for your company. Using Social Connect, shoppers can share their experiences on your site and with your products.

But Social Connect goes beyond sharing. ShopSocially enables merchants to access conversion rates on the links shared, the number of clicks, and other important metrics. This information is extremely valuable because it lets you know in an instant how successful your sales and other promotional campaigns are doing.

Businesses can also monetize their fan base by creating a Shoppers community, which is the merchant's Facebook fan page. This is the place where fans can see what their friends and other shoppers are buying from the merchant. The Shoppers tab also shows who the top shoppers are for a particular retailer and what top products were purchased.

Social Connect has the potential to drive traffic to your door, thanks to good old-fashioned word of mouth.

Milyoni

People hate watching movies alone. Whether in the theater or in the living room, watching a good (or bad) movie alone diminishes the experience because there's no one to share it with.

In fact, many events in our lives—concerts, movies, and sporting events—are better when shared with friends and family.

Milyoni is a company that gets that concept. Pronounced "million-eye," the tech startup has made quite a name for itself with its Conversational Commerce platform.

This platform consists of four Facebook apps that promote the shared experiences in our lives: Social Cinema, Social Live, Social Giving, and Social Shopping.

Social Giving enables fans of a Facebook page to donate to any cause, sharing features with Social Connect from ShopSocially.

Social Cinema and Social Live, though, offer a unique experience for Facebook users. Imagine having the capability of watching a feature film or concert on Facebook and being able to share comments and observations with fellow Facebook watchers as the event happens.

Milyoni is an example of leveraging social media to make the viewing experience better. But it's also an example of how businesses can get very creative with how they integrate social platforms into their business in new and innovative ways.

That's what the Conversational Commerce product line is all about: taking common experiences and providing businesses with a way to monetize them in those new ways.

Moontoast

Moontoast features customizable storefronts that let you build ecommerce stores right in their existing Web pages or within your Facebook newsfeed.

Moontoast services cover a wide range of customers, although the company has chosen to categorize for groups: retailers, music producers, publishers, and celebrities.

For businesses (or celebrities) that have done the marketing to create big fan bases, Moontoast enables a way to sell "direct to your best consumers," where and when they are actively engaged in the company's brand.

Also, the Moontoast Distributed Store product allows merchants to extend commerce out to various locations, such as topical blogs. This extends commerce to where consumers gather, as opposed to a more traditional model of trying to get consumers to come to your website.

This last group enables celebrities (who are not hurting for a social following because, well, they're celebrities) to take advantage of their social power and push sales of memorabilia or special events, typically to raise money for a charitable organization.

Moontoast is keen on making sure that social participation can be converted to actual sales. Their deep analytics tools make it easy to track how those efforts are doing.

The Last Word

Social commerce tools fall into two main categories: those that assist transactions directly and those that enhance marketing to create more business. In this chapter, we examined just the tip of the iceberg for such tools.

In Chapter 3, "Choosing PayPal for Social Media," you will see how easy it is to set up and run the PayPal transaction tools featured in this chapter, so you can get started right away with your own social commerce plan.

3

Choosing PayPal for Social Media

As social media participation grows, the characteristics of all our different cultures are starting to come through with regard to art, music, language, and commerce. When we share ideas, we also want to share things that are related to those ideas.

For example, when someone describes a picture that she likes, you might like to have a copy of that picture, too. So, she posts it on a photo-sharing site and gives you permission to download it for your own use—perhaps to post on your desktop background or print for your office.

But if the shared object in question is something that is not free, say, perhaps a piece of art that should be bought to support the artist, then you and your friend will need a way to exchange the item that involves some sort of transaction.

Isn't This a Wallet?

It may not make sense, at first, why PayPal is exploring ways of getting into social media. After all, when all is said and done, PayPal is fundamentally just a wallet. A super-cool, hyper-secure, fancy wallet, to be sure, but a wallet nonetheless: it holds money for when you need to pull that money out and pay someone for something.

What's social media about that?

Actually, it turns out to be quite a bit about social media.

Commerce Is *Not* the Goal

The first major opportunity for understanding PayPal's presence in the social media ecosystem is an idea touched on in the previous chapter: social media is about communication, not commerce.

On the highest level, this is very true. When talking to your friends face-to-face, very often the idea of buying and selling items does not come up. In fact, if any item is to be given, your friends are typically very reluctant to charge anything for it. They are friends, after all, and giving them something they need that you have is just being, well, a friend.

But sometimes your friends need more than what you can give them freely. You can spend time fixing a computer for a friend, but you can't typically buy him a new computer. What you can do, however, is recommend a place you know where he can get a decent machine for a good value.

This, then, is where commerce starts to creep into the conversation. As you will see in Chapter 4, "Mapping the Social Media Landscape and Key Websites," there are successful sites solely dedicated to the notion of sharing information and reviews about stores and businesses. These sites bridge the gap between commercial and social. But "commerce" can take a more beneficial form, too.

There are those terrible times when your friends need a lot of help, more than what you can ordinarily do. So you perform extraordinary tasks to assist them: you pass the hat around and raise money; you give them food, shelter, clothing; you do whatever it takes to help them get back on

Figure 3.1
Sometimes disasters mean pulling together massive resources.

their feet (see **Figure 3.1**). Organizing this kind of emergency relief involves talent, time, and money (another place where ecommerce enters the conversation).

So, while you can see that commerce is not the primary goal of most of the conversations with those with whom you have close relationships, it can enter the conversation in natural ways every day.

Broadening Your Horizons

In a face-to-face conversation, it can be awkward to include commercial elements in the conversation. But social media has added something to the equation that changes the very notion of "community" as we know it.

This week alone, you may have online conversations with friends in England, Australia, Canada…or any nation on the planet. These are friends you have met in person maybe once or twice, and for some people, you may have never met them. But, nonetheless, they are your friends, and you treat them accordingly. You exchange ideas within the context of your professional careers, and also without. You learn new things about the communities in which they live, and hopefully they learn more about yours.

This is what social media and the Internet before it have done to the idea of relationships: together, they have broadened the scope to the degree that each and every one of us can reach out and establish a connection with the 1.5 billion people on the planet who are connected to the Internet.

There are limitations, naturally, and language is a big one. All of your friends may be English-speaking, with a smattering of German or French speakers that perhaps you can follow. Communication still relies on having a common language, while translation sites can help get basic ideas across.

The expansion of the number of people with which you can communicate is bound to have a significant impact on the types of conversations you have because of the sheer diversity of skills and talent of the larger group of people in the social group.

For instance, if you're at a small party and accidentally cut your finger, then asking "Is there a doctor in the house?" might be kind of silly (unless all of your friends were doctors). But if you ask the same question in a crowd of people, the odds that there is a doctor or nurse or EMT in the crowd goes up significantly.

That's what the *broadening* of the horizons means: if you need something really specific, the odds go up that someone in the larger group will be able to supply you with what you need—or point you directly to someone who can.

This is why businesses are so keen to be part of social media: they know that if they can start being a part of the normal conversations that fill our daily lives, then the chances are greater that someone will need something that they can offer. Once that happens, the conversation can shift, hopefully naturally, into a trade or purchase for goods and services.

NOTE: The ability to turn a conversation into a transaction is a tricky business, and Part III, "A Social Media Sales Playbook," will deal specifically with ideas on how to accomplish this.

This is not trying to paint a picture of a social media landscape where someone will interject commercials every five seconds. But with a wider world participating in social media activities, it will not be unheard of for transactions to enter the picture.

Where PayPal Fits in Social Media

It's obvious why PayPal wants to be a part of the social media equation. If transactions are indeed going to be an inevitable outcome of social media conversations, then having a secure and proven method of conducting those transactions becomes all that much more important.

Security

The first benefit to using PayPal in a social media context is that it provides a layer of security for anyone with whom you're working.

If you are selling a friend something, you want to make sure that her transaction is safer, because you don't want anything to go wrong and jeopardize your relationship. For face-to-face transactions, that's not terribly difficult, since there's typically a lot of trust in such arrangements. When your friend hands you a check, you don't usually try to verify it. You just give her the item and deposit the check. If something were to go wrong, because that's how life works sometimes, then you are confident your friend will fix it.

PayPal INSIDER

Working with Social Media

Social media might not seem like an ideal fit with PayPal at first. After all, the main notion of social media platforms is all about sharing everything, while PayPal is about keeping information about financial dealings tightly held.

So how does this work? In short, PayPal is introducing tools that will act as a private layer for socially based financial transactions. Thus, the conversation around the transaction can be open, but the transaction itself will be maintained with all of the security and privacy one expects from PayPal.

When you're selling to someone who is far away, or you don't know that person all that well, extra precautions are necessary—because you don't know her, and she doesn't know you either.

In these cases, it's best to use an agreed-upon method of payment that both sides can trust. This is where PayPal is most effective. Its security methodology is designed to make sure that everyone involved in a transaction is as protected as possible (see **Figure 3.2**).

Figure 3.2
Take a look at PayPal's security procedures.

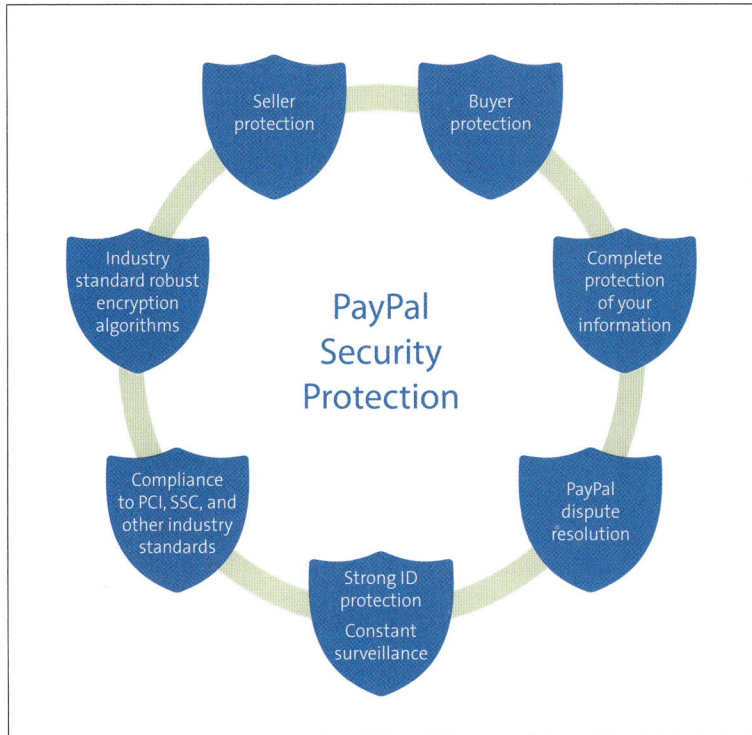

Seller protection

Buyer protection

Complete protection of your information

PayPal
Security
Protection

Industry standard robust encryption algorithms

Compliance to PCI, SSC, and other industry standards

PayPal dispute resolution

Strong ID protection
Constant surveillance

Convenience

Another reason why PayPal is appropriate for use in social media transactions is that it's convenient to use. It doesn't take a lot of time to set up a PayPal customer account, and it doesn't take much longer to set up a merchant account. You can add ecommerce functionality to your site with relative ease and be up and running in hours.

Once configured, the smooth PayPal transaction process highlighted in Chapter 1 makes it easy for anyone to jump from a conversation directly to a transaction.

NOTE: For more information on merchant products and services, visit **www.paypal.com/webapps/mpp/merchant.**

The Last Word

Because of the growing nature of the conversations that social media is bringing to your door, the need to have a secure and convenient way to implement transactions when they arise is an important part of the process.

In Chapter 4, "Mapping the Social Media Landscape and Key Websites," we will look at just how this big social media conversation appears now, so you can have a better idea of where you can fit within the conversation.

Part 2

CHOOSING SOCIAL MEDIA PRESENCE

4

Mapping the Social Media Landscape and Key Websites

The social media landscape has grown far beyond sites like Facebook and MySpace. All sorts of social sites and mobile apps are available to enable communication through words, images, and videos. While nearly all social media outlets encourage connections through some kind of interaction, the content of that communication—the currency, if you will—can change, depending on what service you are using. Before exploring how to capitalize on social media for your business, it's best to familiarize yourself with the social media landscape.

The key thing to do when looking around the social media landscape is to listen. Hear what people are taking about and what interests them. You may learn about something new before it becomes the next best thing since sliced bread.

Getting the Lay of the Land

What's interesting about media is that it was always a part of our social lives. People talk, people listen…sounds pretty social to us. But until recently, all media was a one-way proposition. The ascension of sites like Facebook, YouTube, Twitter, and Flickr has brought us true social media: a huge, always-on conversation using text and multimedia that anyone can watch and join.

All of these social media sites, and others, are more than just fun ways to share your life with friends and family (though they're good at that, too). Social media provides an incredible outlet for your business to reach your customers. Just as communication between a business and its customers used to be one-way and one-dimensional—you placed ads, you talked to customers individually—businesses now have the capability to connect to as many customers as they'd like, using tailor-made messaging that can reach their audience on personal computers and smartphones.

More importantly, the conversation is now two-way. You can talk to your customers, and they can talk to you. Sometimes that conversation isn't always fun, but it's an honest part of your business, and with the right tools and attention, even the most disgruntled customers can become allies if they know you're listening.

Each social media site offers these conversations in its own way, using content as the currency of communications exchange. Many times that currency is the written word, but sometimes it's video, music, or images.

In money, currencies all work the same: you give someone something with value to receive something back of equivalent value. So it is with social media: no matter what the currency of the content, the trading of knowledge and shared lives is really what's going on. To use it best for your business, all you need to do is use the right currency.

Make Friends with Facebook

By now, the story of Mark Zuckerberg's creation of arguably the most popular social media site on the planet is well ingrained in our culture: young, brilliant, and ambitious college student founded a website in 2004 originally intended to give Harvard and other college students a way of tracking their classmates.

The site, Facebook, would go on to dominate the social media landscape and indeed the Internet itself, providing an easy-to-use portal for all levels of users. This ease-of-use helped enable users of any technical skill set to congregate and share news, photos, and videos about themselves as well as participate in shared experiences like games and surveys.

Because of its one-stop-shopping nature, there are many Facebook users who do not wander much beyond the virtual walls of the Facebook site, save to view the occasional link offered up from friends and colleagues. This, more than anything else, is the biggest draw for businesses and advertisers looking to reach out to Facebook's own estimated 750 million users (250 million of them mobile users), who are spending 700 billion minutes a month on Facebook, which comes out to the equivalent of 1.3 million person-years. Per month.

PayPal INSIDER

PayPal's Relationship with Facebook

Facebook has quickly emerged as one of PayPal's largest customers, generating millions of dollars in Transaction Processing Volume (TPV) and revenue. PayPal is offered as a payment option for both Facebook Credits and Facebook Ads. Facebook Credits is Facebook's virtual currency that can be used to play games and acquire digital goods on the Facebook network. In addition, Facebook Credits can also be used to purchase other digital media, such as movies and music.

Facebook Ads offers users and merchants the ability to expand their customer bases by using PayPal to purchase advertising space on the Facebook network, giving them access to Facebook's community of over 750 million users.

Facebook's social media currency is as broad as it comes. When it was first launched, it was all about the easily updated user status. Then it was messaging and news feeds dedicated to the user's friends. Photos were always a part of the Facebook experience, but later videos would be added. The latest feature addition to Facebook is video calls.

Because of the dynamic nature of Facebook, software developers are able to plug their own additions into Facebook. The most well-known examples involve the games that populate the Facebook ecosystem. But these add-ons also contain a large number of business-oriented tools—including PayPal, business pages, and SlideShare—that can be used to enhance your customers' experiences immediately.

NOTE: There are many great Facebook apps available for business…the landscape is ever-changing. A search on any search engine for "Facebook business apps" will yield the latest information on what's out there.

PayPal is one such business that has a business page on Facebook (www.facebook.com/paypal), demonstrating one way that such a page can connect to customers.

With such a wide variety of communication methods available, Facebook is nearly the perfect place to get started on a social media campaign.

Direct Your Action on YouTube

With few exceptions, most social media sites have a narrow way of enabling user communication and sharing. But "narrow" doesn't mean "limited," as you will plainly see.

YouTube is a great example of how diverse a single line of communication can be. Launched in 2005, YouTube provides users with an easy way to upload and store their personal or professional videos for all the world to see.

The site became (and has remained) a huge success for many reasons, partly due to the simplicity of its function and partly because video capture technology has become so widely available. Dedicated video cameras are relatively inexpensive, and it's impossible these days to find a cell phone *without* a video camera. Couple that with an easy-to-use site, and it's easy to see there's your instant hit.

NOTE: YouTube has a special place in PayPal's heart, as the popular video site was founded by three former PayPal employees: Steve Chen, Chad Hurley, and Jawed Karim.

The business implications of YouTube are very strong and have many benefits: imagine creating marketing materials and uploading them to the video-hosting site. But it can go further than that because videos can be used to educate customers on how to use products or connect customers to staff members, store locations, or special promotions.

You can also plug YouTube functionality into your website, letting your website visitors see and even upload videos directly to your company's YouTube channel. This feature gives your business the capability of running things like video contests from within YouTube or from your own website.

Twitter Your Business

Twitter is part of a movement called microblogging. Twitter is another example of "narrow" content, as it involves the written word only, and downsizes it even further—you only get 140 characters per message (or "tweet"). Millions of people have taken this reductionism to a whole new level, conveying many ideas and messages in their tweets.

Or, said in Twitter-speak: Twitter, microblogging can boggle. Text-only, with just 140 characters/tweet. With right skills, though, many ideas and messages can be sent.

NOTE: "Going viral" doesn't mean a case of the cooties, but that transcendental experience obtained when your social media content is shared exponentially across the Internet. It is, in social media terms, awesome.

The idea behind Twitter's creation was simple: enable phone text messages to be shared and displayed on the Web. Because of texting's 140-character limit, the same limitation was applied to Twitter messages. Tweets are read mostly by a Twitter user's followers, though the general public can view tweets as well, especially if a particular tweet is retweeted and shared virally throughout the network.

The nature of tweets is like any other human conversation. Much of the information being shared may be rather useless, except to the person doing the tweeting ("Eating breakfast. Cheese omelet."). On the other hand, it can be informative, such as breaking news, or in some cases actual live posts from historical events, like the Arab Spring protests in 2011.

NOTE: Tweets can be imbued with hashtags (#), which enable tweets to be organized around specific news, people, or events. In this way, a Twitter user can follow and participate in an extended conversation on the Olympics, for example, by setting up a filter to view all messages tagged with #olympics.

Businesses have adopted Twitter in two primary ways: first, as a way to broadcast marketing messages, and second, to communicate directly with customers about their concerns. If a customer is following a business, for instance, the customer could add the Twitter ID for the business in their message, which the business will see as a "mention." Smart businesses pay attention to hashtags and mentions that refer to them, so they can respond quickly to customers' issues.

NOTE: Not every business uses multiple Twitter accounts to handle communications; often, a single account is more than enough to handle conversations with your customers.

...And The Rest

Facebook, Twitter, and YouTube are by no means the only social media sites in existence; they are simply very popular at this time. But there are other sites out there that deserve inspection, because your business may have some use for them.

Google Plus (or +)

Google Plus, also known as Google+, is the latest social media network to hit the scene. Currently, the site is in beta mode, with use of the site by invitation only. As soon as it went live, use of the site exploded, reaching 20 million users in just a couple of weeks, according to several technology news outlets at the time.

Google+ primarily uses the user's written comments as its social currency, but adds geolocation, photo and video uploads, and link sharing as early features. One attraction for Google+ users is its instant-update functionality and the way that connections are managed through specific categories of connection types, known as *circles*.

Businesses should keep an eye on Google+, not just because it's the latest cool thing but also because Google+ will have complete integration with all other Google products.

This means that Google+ will be tightly matched with the millions of Android phone users out there. Android phone users already can upload photos instantly from their phone cameras and make use of geolocation features. Just imagine what businesses could tap into when allowed to add their functionality and presence to Google+.

Flickr

Flickr is a photo-sharing site that enables users to share their photos and videos with other users.

The Yahoo!-owned Flickr provides a great way for any user—personal or commercial—to easily host huge galleries of images free of cost. Businesses looking to host pictures for an online catalog or from a business event, for instance, would benefit from a Flickr account.

Vimeo

Vimeo provides users with an easy way to upload and store their personal or professional videos. One advantage to Vimeo is it doesn't impose a time duration on the length of videos users can post.

Business that are looking to produce a lot of video content might want to examine Vimeo as a possible social media platform.

WordPress

WordPress is one of the premier blogging platforms in the world, and it provides two key blogging services for its users.

The first is blogging software that can be downloaded and installed to work with a separate website, such as a business site. This software is free to use and very popular.

Social Media SUCCESS STORY

C'est Cheese: Exploring Social Media

Mari's first challenge is to figure out which social networks her company should use to connect to her customers. She's already decided to use PayPal for her online payment system, and wants to use the tools that she's heard will connect directly with those networks, too. But she doesn't want to be limited to those networks alone.

Given the relative age of her customers, middle age and older, Mari is pretty sure that Facebook is going to be a good network to use to plug into those customers. But she would like to catch younger customers who are just exploring culinary products and good food as well, and isn't sure which options provide the best payoff for this group.

A lot of her customers have expressed an interest in cooking classes, but Mari's store doesn't have the right kind of space for that. Instead, she is thinking about producing some videos that will demonstrate how to cook with some of her store's products, so she definitely will want a YouTube account.

Along the same lines as cooking classes, posting some recipes on a blog would work, too. Her store's website is already set up to be an online catalog, and she doesn't want to spend money for a redesign to add a blog. What she can do, though, is set up a free blog on WordPress.com and create a link to that blog from her main website.

Mari will take a look at where her customers can be found as the story continues in Chapter 6, "Connecting with Social Media Customers."

The second and more of a social media service is the blog hosting provided on WordPress.com. On this site, users can set up and start entering their own blog entries—again, completely free of charge.

Hosting your business blog on WordPress is a great solution for businesses that may not have a website yet or (more likely) a website that isn't entirely configured to host a blog. The massive WordPress community can share your content (that it likes) and really get the word out fast, too.

The Last Word

Social media is a landscape that is constantly in flux, so the sites mentioned here can change, in mission, audience, or even existence. However, they are well known as the bellwethers of social media, and can provide your company with great ways to reach out to customers of all walks of life.

In Chapter 5, "Planning Your Social Media Brand Presence," you will begin the process of figuring out how to enter these various aspects of social media. Just because you know what they are doesn't mean you can enter social networks without a plan.

5

Planning Your Social Media Brand Presence

It's very tempting, now that you've seen all the social media platforms out there, to just jump on and start tweeting, friending, and liking everyone in sight. Spread the word about your business and the customers will start flocking in, right?

Well, don't be so quick on the draw, pardner. Leaping into social media without a plan or strategy is about as smart as running into a crowded room and yelling aloud about your business or organization to everyone in the room. Yes, you will definitely get their attention, but it may not be the kind of attention you want.

The Whys of Strategy

There are three major reasons why you shouldn't start broadcasting information about you and your organization willy-nilly on the various social media platforms.

The first, which was hinted at in the chapter introduction, is that it would be silly—to the point of being embarrassing. Your parents' advice about thinking before you speak definitely holds true in social media, because, in general, what you say in cyberspace can and will be remembered (and recalled) for a long time.

Thinking before you speak or otherwise engage people on the Internet is also important because it takes a long time to build good relationships, but just a few ill-chosen words to damage a relationship irreparably. This is reason number one why you should have a strategy in place for social media.

If this sounds a bit calculating, let's put it in another perspective. You would not walk into a preschool class, for instance, and start talking about particle physics, would you? The same thing holds true for speaking to your social media audience; you need to have a plan in place that at least figures out the parameters of what you will say and how you will say it.

Secondly, you need to know what your overall message will be. This is just business common sense—if you have a marketing and advertisement strategy in place already, you don't want to throw a wrench into it and start delivering another message entirely. The strongest message is the most coordinated message.

Finally, it's very important to recognize that like most technology, tools will change, and often very quickly. All of the tools highlighted in Chapter 4, "Mapping the Social Media Landscape and Key Websites," could very well be obsolete in a year's time, or even less. That's the nature of technology. So, if you make your plan around one or two platforms ("We're going to launch a Twitter-only campaign."), you may be in for a rude surprise if Twitter were ever to close down. There are a lot of tools out there, as seen in **Figure 5.1**.

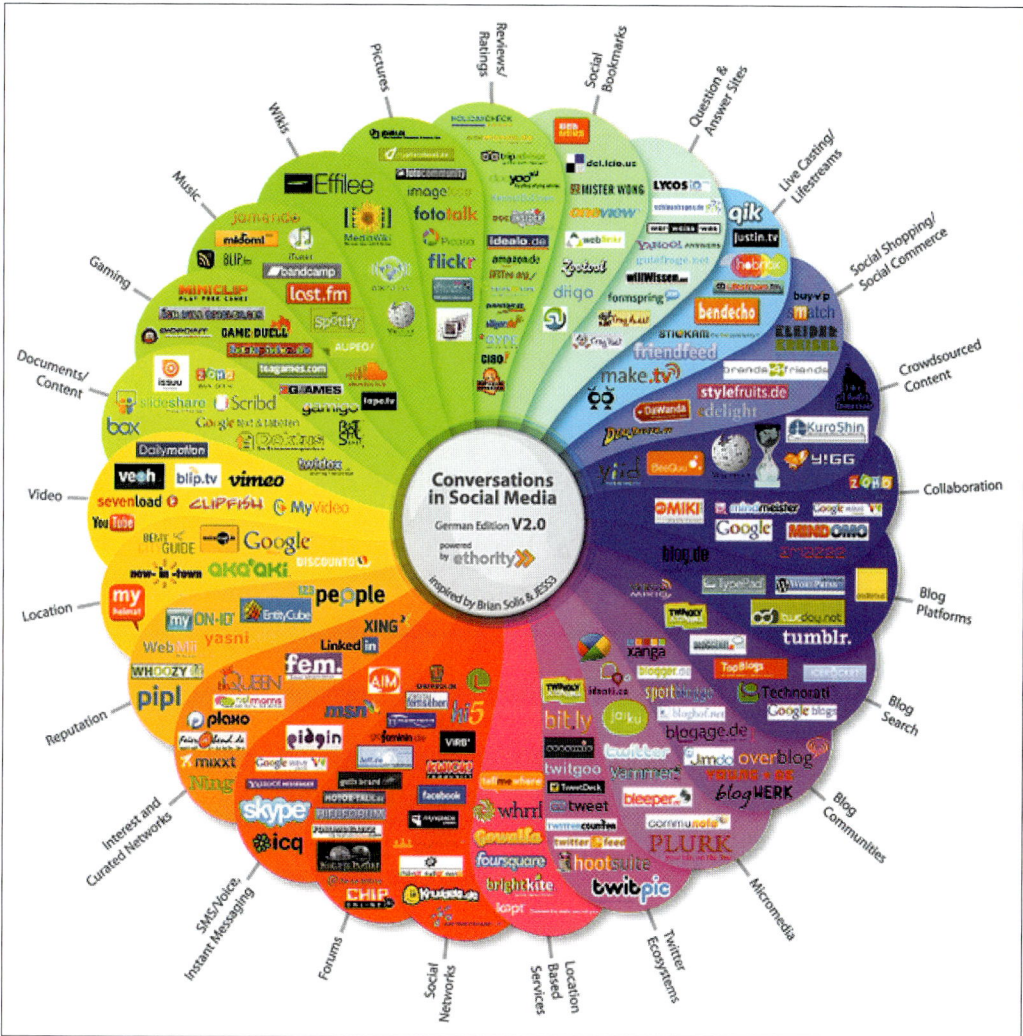

Figure 5.1 *The current state of social media reveals a lot of complexity.*

Better, then, to craft a plan that delivers a message or set of messages that you want to convey and then push those messages out on the platforms where your customers are. If that happens to be only Twitter, then fine. But you need to bring the conversation to your customers on whatever site or sites they are using.

Setting Goals

The very first item on your agenda is to set the goals for your social media strategy. Without goals, not only will your message be all over the map, but you will also find it difficult to measure success if you have no idea what it is you want to achieve in the first place.

What's Your Message?

This question may seem blatantly obvious, but it's key for getting started with any social media plan. What is the message of your company? What is its story? Believe it or not, people will be interested because they like a good story.

Think about what your company does and how it got to this point. You may think it was all one gigantic mess—a series of accidental good and bad breaks that somehow led you to where you are. But try to put aside your self-consciousness and look at your company objectively. You may find that how others see your company is different than how you see it.

You may find that your customers are impressed with what you've accomplished, so you can share what you've done with pride. Or you could discover the reverse: customers have an opposite perception of your company than you do, and it's not a pleasant perception.

Don't be discouraged; it just means you have more work to do getting out the message of your company. It also means you will need to retool the aspects in your business that are causing the negative reactions, and quickly. It does little good to set up customers' expectations in social media messaging and then fail to deliver on those expectations when they actually step inside your doors. In fact, it would quickly cause them to lose their trust, which is something you don't want, ever.

Why Are You Doing This?

This may seem to be the same question as determining the goals, but actually it involves a more specific focus of the question: What is the immediate goal of what you want to achieve with your social media messaging? Is it to drive more sales? Strengthen more loyalty among your current customers? Or is this going to be a flat-out marketing campaign?

You could say "all of the above," but to have a more focused message, you should think about choosing just one goal. It will help you measure your results later.

How's Your Relationship?

Don't worry, we're not trying to get personal here. What you need to ask is: How is your relationship with your social network? And by this, we mean your existing customers and the potential customers you are trying to reach.

Have they ever heard of you? Have they been in your store but just the one time? Are they repeat customers? If you're a start-up, who is it you're trying to reach?

Knowing who the members of the network are that you're trying to reach is a very key step in determining your goals. A loyalty program should be aimed at repeat customers, not people who have never heard of your business.

Where Is Your Network?

To reach out to your network, it's important to know where they are in the wilds of the Internet. Are they a younger, more tech-savvy crowd? Then it's likely they're pretty much everywhere that early technology adopters can be found.

If that's the case, then you can try cutting-edge promotions, like photo and video contests, because that crowd will have the knowledge and desire to participate in such events.

If your network is older, then you may need to stick with the platforms that are more contained, such as Facebook, which has an ease-of-use and self-contained quality that currently attracts older adults.

How Will You Tell Your Stories?

To connect with people the best way possible, you will need to have genuine conversations with them. This means dropping the corporate-speak and talking to people. Don't just try to protect your company's image, or put spin on events. Put your best face forward, and make it an honest face.

It won't be easy; you'll be drawn to staying professional and will come off as stiff. Or you'll go too far and reveal too much information. A balance will have to be achieved to make this work. A great example was Old Spice's 2010 social media campaign, which created over 180 video responses to Twitter comments and garnered 22,500 comments and 5.9 million views—in the first 48 hours (http://mashable.com/2010/07/15/old-spice-stats/).

That kind of campaign is beyond most companies' budgets, but you can achieve real connections with your audience with some creativity and thought.

And patience will need to be a big part of your interactions, because not every conversation you have with your network will be pleasant. Don't try to spin your way out of a jam—be honest and own up to any mistakes you might have made. Offer ways for customers to interact with you, don't just shut them down. People will appreciate honesty.

PayPal INSIDER

Telling Your Story

Blogs, social networking sites, ratings, and reviews—these all hold great potential for getting the attention of consumers. Viral marketing can be highly effective, as consumers today are much more likely to trust the recommendations of friends and bloggers than they are to buy into your advertising campaign.

Whatever social media and networking tools you use, we recommend you be sure to do your homework first. Your media must match your customer base. If your target customer fits into a certain social networking sweet spot, the sky is the limit. Get creative, think outside the box, and invite your customers to do some of the hard work of evangelizing for you.

How Will You Succeed?

Before starting your social media plan, you will need to know how you'll ultimately define success. This means taking quantitative measurements of the impact of your messaging, a process known as *analytics.*

Analytics will enable you to measure, for instance, how many people viewed your latest blog post on your website or clicked on that link to a coupon in your Facebook page.

There are many analytics tools out there, such as Google Analytics and SugarCRM, that we'll examine in Chapter 11, "Evaluating Your Social Media Success." It's important that you settle on the right tools before you begin your social media efforts so you can measure your success once the plan is implemented.

Do the Legwork

After you have done the strategic planning of getting your goals and audience ascertained, now it's time to start thinking tactics. Here, finally, is where you should start figuring out which social media platforms to use.

Presumably, you have discovered who your primary audience is and have a good idea of what technology they are using or could be using. Put together a list of social media outlets where you believe you can best connect with people. It can be any number of outlets—blogs, Facebook, Twitter, Google+—but if there are a lot on your list, you may need to whittle the list down to something more manageable.

Once the list is put together, do your legwork by going out to the social media networks and reading. And then read some more. Find out if and how people are talking about you on those networks. What are they saying? Is it good or bad? What are they saying about your competition?

Start-ups can also approach this task with their own goals in mind. Even if you don't have customers yet, you know who your customers should be, and also whom your competitors' customers are. You just need to apply these principles to them.

This is equivalent to listening to a conversation at a party first before jumping in. Doing this will give you an idea of how to fine-tune your message, and give you possible opening lines in the conversation you will eventually be starting with these people.

Bootstrap the Conversation

While you are examining the conversation that's going on in these social media sites, look for people who seem well versed in your business and its interests. If you run a non-profit food bank, for instance, look for key conversationalists around the topics of hunger and poverty. They're out there, for any topic. Just find the people to whom everyone else seems to be listening.

Once you find them, seek what these people have to say. It will give you talking points on what's of interest in your field so you can deliver your own content later. It will also give you insight into who's who in your industry, and perhaps even connect you with influencers who can talk up your organization and help spread the word faster.

Join Conversations

Now it's time to join the conversation. At first, you might be tempted to simply broadcast all that you think is cool about your organization—its product, its people, its brand—all the things you love about your company. That's a common place to start, but understand that if you keep doing that, the novelty will wear off quickly.

Remember, this is always a conversation, no matter what type of social media platform you're working with. That means it can't be a one-way broadcast of just the aspects of your business you find interesting. Be prepared to engage your audience, just as you would if they were in your store.

When you do this, you'll tap into what's cool about social media: you're holding a conversation with someone, but everyone else can listen in. If the conversation ends well, people will look at this and think that you must have a business that's interested in the needs of its customers.

Meanwhile, you will need to offer compelling points of interest so people will seek to converse with you. This might be content on your blog or other social outlet, but it won't be a broadcast, because that would be counter-productive. You will need to strike a balance between talking and listening, with the understanding that people will mostly want to learn from and listen to you, but they will expect to be heard when they do have something to tell you.

Reach Out Beyond Social

"Beyond social," in this case, means beyond the monitor screen you use when conducting social media conversations. In other words, get out there and meet people.

If they don't come to your store (or website or app), go see them. If there are local interest groups that pertain to your organization in any way, attend their meetings. Look for events both locally and out of town, particularly ones where industry influencers might be attending. Seek out such events and put faces with names.

Letting people put a face with your name goes a long way toward building stronger relationships.

Get the Metrics

When you were setting goals, you were also deciding on how you would measure your success. Now that your plan is in action, start measuring. Keep track of your site traffic, Twitter retweets, and Facebook activity— with an eye on all the goals you decided you would need to make this social media outreach a success.

As you go, analyze your metrics. Where did things succeed, and where did they flop? You will soon learn to keep going on the ideas that worked, and you can drop those that failed.

You should never set a plan in motion and then stick to the plan blindly. Be ready to adapt to new and unforeseen circumstances. They will crop up, and if you're ready to roll with them, you'll come out in great shape.

The Last Word

In this chapter, you learned some of the key points in planning a social media presence for your organization. We only scratched the surface of what a good social media plan should be.

Starting in Chapter 6, "Connecting with Social Media Customers," we'll discuss the actual tactics mentioned in this chapter, beginning with a look at how to find out who your customers are and where they might be engaged in social media.

Part 3

A SOCIAL MEDIA SALES PLAYBOOK

6

Connecting with Social Media Customers

It's the age-old problem for business owners: in order to sell to customers, you have to first find customers. In pre-electronic times, it was simpler: hang your shingle out on a storefront, and if your goods and services were good and your prices fair, then the customers would come through the door.

Today, it's harder. With more competition and customers spread out all over town, or even the world, it's harder than ever to find people with whom to do business. In this chapter, we'll show you exactly how to go about seeking and finding your audience within social media—an audience that may one day become paying customers or active participants in your organization.

First Things First

Before you begin to look for your social media audience, it's important to set a few ground rules for your search. When looking for any item, it's easy to make the mistake of having unreasonable expectations and ultimately finding the wrong thing.

You have your overall strategy in place, so you know where you want to go and what you want to do with social media. Now you should apply that strategy to the very beginning of your plan.

Make Time

Okay, let's just get this out of the way, right up front: this is going to take time.

It would be nice if we could magically wave a few paragraphs at you and give you the fast way to find a social media audience. But there isn't a magic formula to do it instantly, and anyone who tells you differently may also have a certain bridge to sell you.

But the good news is that it's not hard to do…just time-consuming.

The first thing you need to do is schedule time for your social media. Don't just "get to it when you get to it." Instead, really figure out a time and place where you will work on your social media plan and stick with it.

To help yourself, make sure you cut down on the distractions. Focus on what you're doing in that moment. If you're writing a blog, then focus on that until it's done. Don't get pulled away by tasks that can be done later. This is now part of your job, and it deserves the appropriate amount of attention. This will vary, of course, depending on your business and its needs, but you will need to spend more than just a day or two on social media, that's for sure.

Also, make sure that you understand you're in for the long haul. Social media isn't a sprint, it's a marathon. Peak too early, and you'll collapse from "social exhaustion." Lose your discipline, and you won't reach your goal.

Of course, there are ways to help yourself use less time. One way to do that is by finding people with whom to connect.

Find Relevant Content

You can leverage the knowledge of people and organizations that have been in your shoes. They're the experienced ones, the thought leaders and knowledge managers of your particular interest or business sector.

They're also great resources for getting started in social media, and as such, great time savers.

There are three reasons why tracking down relevant content and the producer of that content will be good for you.

- **You can hear where the conversation is.** Social media is all about conversations. And thankfully (or not), the conversation on the Internet never ends. Whatever your business—model trains, cheese making, office supplies—you can bet there's someone out there who has an opinion on it. And those opinionated people will have people who listen to them. It could be thousands of followers, or just dozens, but the important consideration is they have captured the attention of others. So what are those opinion holders saying? Is it relevant to you and your business? Do people agree with them, and do you agree with them?

  You don't have to agree with them, but you do need to hear what they have to say so you can determine what topics are important. You may have other topics in mind, of course, and that's great—you may be able to start some conversations of your own.

- **If you listen to thought leaders, your customers might, too.** If you are in a particular business, and there are thought leaders in the same field, it's a good bet that others are listening to these people, too. Other people in the audience may be potential customers or potential competitors. Either way, it doesn't hurt to pay attention to the "crowd" and hear what they have to say.

  You may find someone in your hometown, for example, who is interested in whatever goods and services you have to sell. Reach out to that person and make a connection. If they're an existing customer, great! If they're a potential customer, so much the better.

  If there are competitors in the crowd, listen to what they have to say. They won't likely give away trade secrets, but they might express solutions to problems their business (and perhaps yours) has. If they are fellow business people but in locations too far away to compete, definitely reach out to them and share your ideas and problems.

- **If thought leaders listen to you, your customers will, too.** If you start engaging in the conversation with these thought leaders, you may find that people who are listening to them will start listening to you as well. Don't be pushy about it; people who have established social media audiences can spot an attention-seeker a mile off. Be honest, and say what you need to say because you feel it's important, not because you're trying to work in a plug.

Be Selective

It will be very tempting to just connect to anyone and everyone who happens to meet in social media outlets. After all, the more people with whom you connect, the better the chances of getting more customers, right? Not exactly.

A key component to understand about social media is that not everyone you meet will really be a genuinely helpful connection. This is not meant to disparage anyone in particular, but like any crowd of people you run into, some people will simply be more interesting and more helpful than others.

Typically, you should seek out people who will have a direct connection to or interest in your efforts. As you work on Facebook, Twitter, or any other social media site, hopefully you will be friended or followed by a lot of people. Don't immediately reciprocate. This sounds rather anti-social, but the fact of the matter is, there are people out there who are trying to promote their own business interests and are incorrectly using social media platforms as just another channel for spam messaging. They have nothing relevant to say, other than the desire to promote their own commercial venture.

TIP: If you do get a spam message on a social media site, take the time to report the sender as a spammer. It will help the broader community as a whole.

You don't need to worry about spammers following you on Twitter, or liking a company fan page on Facebook. But you should *not* follow them back, because that's what they need to grow. What's interesting on Twitter is that because of the systematic way these spammers conduct their business, they will almost always stop following you once they see you haven't followed them back after a day or so. This reduces their chances of being reported as a spammer and blocked from Twitter altogether.

If you're reading this and wondering about being perceived as a spammer, don't worry. We're trying to caution you against spammers here. With your well-outlined social media plan, you will not be spamming anyone. We'll discuss this more in Chapter 7, "Transforming Social Relationships into Customers," but the big difference in what spammers do and what you will do is that you'll be offering genuine value in your conversations. By sharing with others your unique knowledge and insights, people should come to respect you and want to conduct business with you.

So Where Are Your Customers?

We've set up the rules of the road a bit, and now it's time to find these people out on the Internet. It will take a little bit of sleuthing, particularly up front, but you will find that the techniques here are not hard to do.

Ask Customers Where They Are

Yes, just asking should be the first thing you do. A lot of business owners assume that there's some special trick to figuring out where their customers reside online. And while there are some ways to find this information on your own, you can do the easy thing first and simply ask.

But what information should you acquire? At the very least, you should get your customers' email addresses. You can use these addresses later to look for them on social media sites. Other key pieces of information you might want could include the following:

- Mailing address
- LinkedIn ID
- Facebook ID
- MySpace ID
- Twitter ID
- *Permission to contact them by mail/email*
- Google Plus ID

The last item on this list cannot be emphasized enough: you *must* get their permission to reach out to them. Quite a few people cherish their privacy and do not want to be on yet another mailing list. So it's important that you give them a chance to opt-in to whatever connection you're trying to establish.

You might wonder why, in a social media book, you need to worry about someone's mailing address. It's because, depending on the demographic of your customers, there may be people who will not be connected to the Internet regularly. More people are connecting to the Internet each passing day, but the number of those who aren't connected is relevant enough to keep in mind.

One way to gather this information might be to give your customers a little mini-survey as they do business with you. Offer them a discount on goods and services if they complete even just a minimum part of the survey. (Another reason to have the mailing address question—it won't leave non-connected users out of a chance to get a discount.)

Social Media SUCCESS STORY

C'est Cheese: Reaching Out

Mari has been successful in asking some customers about their social media activities, but she wants to create more of an outreach.

Seeking a creative way to point out her store's blog, she included the Internet address (known in tech-speak as the *URL*) for the blog on the cheese labels in the cases, and had one of her cheese mongers carve the URL in a big wheel of displayed cheese.

She also went old school and framed a printout of her latest blog entry and set the frame next to the line for the cash register. The content changed every week or so as she updated the blog online. Customers noticed the creative displays of the URL and ended up following the blog regularly because they were interested in what Mari had to say.

In Chapter 9, "Sharing with Rich Media," we'll look at some of the compelling content that Mari was able to offer on her blog and other social media outlets.

However you ask, make sure that the pitch is low pressure. Emphasize that you aren't seeking to send them a bunch of ads, but that you are seeking to make a connection with them. Because that's what you will be doing.

TIP: You can also purchase information from companies that collate demographics for social media. Marketing reports for companies also carry this information, and can provide it

Be Proactive

This rule might be a little too obvious for people so they sometimes miss it, but it's important to advertise that you're out there on the Internet, ready to be followed.

Many are the times we've seen a business stick "Like Us on Facebook" or some similar message on a receipt or a poster. And really, for the amount of time it takes to create such blurbs, there's no reason not to do it.

Another quick way to advertise your social media is to incorporate your social media links within your email signature. This is a quick and easy way to let people know not only that you're "out there" on social media, but also exactly where your business is.

PayPal INSIDER

Connect with Customers' Blogs

The key to social media is building relationships. And to build positive relationships, you need to know your customers. Blogging is a great way to open a dialogue and get insight into what matters to your target audience. It's easy to enter conversations with influential bloggers. By building relationships within this small group, you have the chance to boost awareness about your brand and increase sales. Why? Because consumers trust individual opinions more than mass advertising.

A good rule to follow as you enter the blogging realm is to listen before you leap. Get to know a blog by reading posts before you participate or respond, so you can make sure that your posts are relevant in tone and timing. When you comment on someone else's blog, be transparent about the fact that you're representing a company.

You can also start an executive blog to communicate with your customers. The more you put into it, the more you'll get out of it. If you keep your content fresh and engage visitors, you'll deepen their interest in your brand. An executive blog gives readers an intimate, immediate experience with your company, which helps build lasting relationships.

A slick way of accomplishing this is to actually add icons of the social media platforms you're on to the signature of your emails. It's less cluttered than just providing links.

There are two ways you can use such icons: you can link them to your own social media accounts, so people can click them and follow or like your business. Or you can link the icons to the generic home pages of these services, which will enable users to immediately share the content of your email with their followers. The decision should really rely on what kind of content you send out via email. If it's very transactional ("your donation was received," "your order was shipped"), then just link to your own accounts. If you use it to send out newsletters and other useful content on a regular basis, use these icons to encourage recipients to share the content on their social networks.

Let's see how to do this in Gmail, keeping in mind that the solution will be similar in other Web-based and desktop mail client applications. For this example, a link will be created to personal Web pages and specific social media connections.

1. Download the icons you need. There are a lot of places on the Internet to find such artwork. Just type "social media icons" into your favorite search engine, and you'll find an abundance of such art, available for free.

2. After the icons are saved to your computer, Gmail will only be able to access them from another website, not as a file on your computer. An easy option is to upload the images you want to use back to the Images section of your Google Docs account. In your browser, navigate to http://docs.google.com.

3. Click the Upload button and select the Files option. An Open File dialog will appear.

4. Find and select the images of the icons you want to use and click Choose.

5. If the Upload settings dialog appears, click Start Upload.

6. Navigate to the image in the Images and Videos section of Google Docs.

7. Click the Share link in the Upload Complete box. The Sharing Settings dialog will open.

8. Click the Change link in the Sharing Settings dialog. The Visibility Options screen will appear.

9. Select the Public on the Web option and click Save.

10. Click Done. The Sharing Settings dialog will close.

11. Repeat Steps 3–10 to upload icons as needed.

Now that the icons are stored in a place where anyone with a Web browser can access them, you can easily add them to your Gmail signature.

1. Click the icon in Google Docs. The icon will open.

2. Right-click the icon and select the Copy Image Address option.

3. In Gmail, click the Settings icon and select the Mail Settings option. The Settings page will open to the General tab.

4. Scroll to the Signature section.

5. Click the Insert Image icon. The Add an Image dialog will open.

6. Paste the URL of the image link into the Image URL field. The image should appear in the Preview window.

7. Click OK. The Add an Image dialog will close, and the icon will appear in the Signature.

8. Select the icon in the Edit window and click the Link button. The Edit Link dialog will open.

9. Fill out the fields as needed and click OK.

10. Click OK again. The Edit Link dialog will close.

11. Repeat Steps 1–10 as needed.

12. When finished, click the Save Changes button at the bottom of the Gmail settings page.

After your changes are complete, your signature will have a much more graphic look.

Digging on Your Own

You can, with relative ease, also use the social media platform's own tools to find out who's on that platform. All you need are the email addresses of your customers.

If you're using Gmail, Yahoo!, Hotmail, or MSN Messenger for your business email service, for example, you can have the social media service tap into those contacts and see who is already on that service.

When you do this, you should make sure that you are tracking your business email account, not your personal account. While your friends are likely important to your business, it's better to start with known customers first and have your friends jump in on their own later. It helps keep your personal and business lives separate, and doesn't take your friends for granted.

To connect email contacts to your Facebook account, follow these steps.

1. In Facebook, click the Friend Requests menu and select the Find Friends link. The Friends page will open.

2. Click the appropriate source of contact information.

3. Enter your account information and click Find Friends.

4. Facebook will log into the account and search for existing Facebook users.

5. Select the members you would like to invite to be friends of your business.

6. Click Add Friends. The Invite Friends screen will appear.

7. If you would like to invite your email contacts that are not on Facebook yet, you can do so here.

You can also invite contacts from mail services to your Twitter account.

1. In Twitter, click the Who to Follow button. The Who to Follow page will appear.

2. Click the Find Friends tab. The Find Friends tab will appear.

3. Click the Search Contacts button for the service you want to search. The account information dialog for that service will open.

4. Click Grant Access (or similar command), and the search will begin.

5. When the search is complete, click on the accounts of people who matched the email addresses that you want to follow.

The Last Word

As you can see, there are some simple techniques you can use to jump-start the social network for your business. This is not the end of your journey, however, merely the beginning.

While establishing relationships is all good, it's important to remember that you have a purpose driving your connections: getting some business from these relationships. In Chapter 7, "Transforming Social Relationships into Customers," you will learn techniques for converting good social connections into great customers.

7

Transforming Social Relationships into Customers

There is a lot of material out there on how you can effectively convert social media relationships into actual sales. Marketing and Web analysts throw around fancy metric identifiers and terms like *Social Relations Management (SRM)* to replace *Customer Relations Management*. But while SRM and all the hyper-relevant metric tools might have a use for you as your social media efforts grow, let's start with the very basic approaches.

A few of these are the approaches that can work for getting customers whether they're in your place of business, out on the street, or on a social media page on the Internet. They work because a social media relationship is governed by pretty much the same rules that govern other relationships. The rest of the techniques are a little more specialized but common sense all the same.

Listen

We've all seen this before, or maybe been involved in it—an argument between two or more people.

It's easy to stand aside and critique such social fender-benders, particularly after the fact. Many times, it's easy to spot the error: someone wasn't listening.

The reason why listening is so emphasized in social media (other than the fact that listening to any conversation is just plain polite) is that unlike "traditional media," you have to pay far more attention to social media channels. The difference lies in the social nature of this type of media, because you really don't know where, when, or with whom the conversation is going to actually take place.

Contrast this with media that's considered more traditional in nature. Print and broadcast media cycles have patterns: release news to an old-school media outlet and, should it prove interesting enough to the gatekeepers of those outlets (the role filled by editors and reporters), then that news will be published in regular, predictable ways.

With social media, patterns are much, much harder to detect; avoid anyone who tells you otherwise. The truth is, you can put out a whole lot of compelling content, but none of it may be picked up or be considered as interesting by your audience. But put up a toss-away video of a cat dancing at your sister-in-law's wedding, and your video could be the next viral hit of the last 15 minutes.

Hopefully, by following a few simple tips, you should be able to at least listen to conversations enough so that your commentary is relevant.

Know the Crowd

The first thing you need to do is figure out who's talking about you or your business sector. If you're a small business, there may not be a lot of chatter about your company, but you need to make sure.

Visit the social media sites and run a search for your company name. (On Twitter, don't forget to use the hashtag tool. A business named "C'est

Cheese" might be tagged as "#cestcheese," for instance.) You may find there's a conversation going on about your business already. Hopefully it's good, but don't freak out if it's negative. We'll get to that in a bit.

If your business is nowhere to be seen in existing conversations, there's no worry about that, either. Start searching for topics related to your organization, with the idea that whoever is discussing those topics will be of interest to you and your potential audience.

TIP: When searching for thought leaders, it's a good idea to search the general Web first for articles and blog entries written by the people you're trying to find. Searching social media sites first is less efficient.

Hear What's Being Said

Once you locate these conversations, see what they're saying. What's the hot topic right now? Is it directly related to a product or service you provide? How is the tone of the discussion?

These are things that you will need to note as you listen to the conversation. Hold off on responding for a bit…wait a few days and get the lay of the land.

For instance, are your peers in the conversation? What are they saying? You don't necessarily want to parrot them, because you'll sound like someone who's just a "me too" sort of chatterer. Listen to what's being said and by whom. You may find yourself agreeing or disagreeing with a lot of things, so you'll want to take the time to figure out what you're going to say and to whom.

Pay Attention to Where People Are

While most social media is governed by similar rules, there are going to be some places in the context of the conversation that will affect how you will add to the conversation.

If, for instance, your potential audience is mostly responding in comments on the blogs of one or two thought leaders, or even your competition's blogs, then how you jump in the conversation will be trickier.

Blogs are great media for delivering content, but usually a blog entry will set the tone for the conversation to follow. Blog creators (or their moderators) will often be trying to shape the discussion in the direction they want (to drive up their own traffic), and will not brook much (if any) off-topic discussion. If a competitor runs the blog, then that person may be less than forgiving in letting you have any say.

TIP: If you have a blog, let your competition comment on it, unless they're blatantly advertising. Don't be afraid of an open discussion; the audience will appreciate it.

Conversely, on more "open" social mediums, where comments can be more of a free-for-all, you will have the ability to craft your own message in your own terms. Just don't be afraid to listen to others and take their points of view into account.

Timing Is Everything

Conversations on the Internet are often influenced by unforeseen forces.

But then there are the more subtle drivers. For instance, consider the case of a news aggregation/comment site that had a strong traffic drop in the summer, for reasons that weren't immediately apparent. After researching the demographics of the site's readers, the answer jumped out at the site's operators. The site had a huge European presence among professionals, while the U.S. presence was canted toward college students. Summer, therefore, equaled students on break in the U.S. and Europeans taking their extended (by U.S. standards) vacations. After making a concerted effort to engage U.S. professionals (who still wouldn't know what a vacation was if one hit them over the head), the site's summer numbers dipped quite a bit less.

The lesson here is learning what the key drivers are in your business. If you're a retailer, then the annual sales cycles may apply. If you're a non-profit, funding drives will play a key role. Whatever the drivers, learning when the conversation peaks and dips will be very useful information to know.

How to Listen

It's not particularly efficient to check site after site, moving back and forth to try to view the conversations. It can be done, obviously, but you're going to waste a lot of time trying to do it that way.

Better, instead, to use a tool designed to track multiple conversations (and social media outlets) at once. Fortunately, there are not one but two such tools out there: TweetDeck and HootSuite.

TweetDeck is a browser-based Web application that is designed to display multiple streams of social media content. TweetDeck can monitor Twitter, Facebook, LinkedIn, Foursquare, and MySpace accounts and can view multiple streams from any of these accounts. TweetDeck is configured to view the author's Twitter feed in four ways: the current feed, any mentions of the author's Twitter ID, direct messages to the author, and any pending tweets that will go out later.

With TweetDeck you can also configure columns to search for specific terms and track how popular your social media content is. You can even track multiple accounts on the same social media service, such as the Wall content on your personal and business Facebook pages.

HootSuite has similar capabilities. But, in addition, HootSuite can handle social media networks such as Ping.fm, WordPress blogs, and Mixi, and has a tightly integrated analytics package that can help you when you start collecting metrics later.

Be Yourself

Seriously, why even bring this up? Because there is still the notion out there in the business world that you have to spin everything to make it sound as good as you possibly can.

Social media, regardless of what someone might try to tell you, is not about spin. Yes, there are marketing and PR benefits to using social media properly, but that's not the sole focus of social media. If this is your goal in social media, you might want to try something else, because you're going to run into problems right from the get-go.

The reason is simple: people want to have conversations with people, not talking heads with carefully parsed comments. We can identify with people much more easily than a PR statement. If you don't put a real face in the conversation, then your audience will never want to engage with your social media efforts because they know all they will get is market-speak.

Now, being yourself doesn't mean acting like you do at home on the weekend, trudging around in bunny slippers and an old tattered bathrobe while drinking coffee and reading the paper until noon. You still need to put some professionalism into this—just let your personality shine through.

If you're someone with a dry wit, then use that. But be aware that what you think is funny will always have the potential to offend someone, so use humor in moderation.

Above all else, be honest. If you or one of your co-workers makes a customer service error, then own up to it. Publicly. Then work to fix it. People are usually far more willing to work with you if they have a grievance and you take responsibility for the goof.

Have Conversations

You've listened and are itching to get into the conversation. You have a pretty good idea of who's who and what the topics of the moment are. Now it's time to have the conversation.

First, resist the temptation to make an announcement about your social presence. Then succumb to that temptation anyway. While you may want to just dive right in, social media protocol does allow for a little fanfare when you get online. It's expected, and even desired, as long as you don't go overboard.

Next, send an email to your customers, post some bulletins in your store, or put some news on your blog. Wherever you have a presence, make an announcement about your new social media channel. You only get to debut once, so make the most of it.

Once the announcement is out of the way, start easing into the discussions. You don't have to be extraordinarily profound; we can't all be that way 24-7, anyway. But you do need to stay on topic and think a bit before you respond. Nothing kills a conversation faster than something like, "I think you're right, and hey, have you tried Product X? It's only $19.95 at our store."

Actually, that won't kill the conversation so much as turn it against you, fast.

Keep your comments brief, to the point, and as polite as you can. That may not always be easy, but you need to stay cool, no matter what the provocation. Remember, this is part of your job, perhaps even part of your livelihood. Don't lose your temper.

Here are some tips on how to deal with a conversation that's gone negative on you.

- **Find out who's talking.** First, figure out who is being negative. While you don't want anyone being negative about your organization, it is a good idea to prioritize your level of response.

- **Is it a thought leader?** If this is someone with a lot of recognition in your community, then you will need to address their concerns. Likewise if they are a known customer. But if the person is one of those people who likes to complain or antagonize everyone about everything (euphemistically known as a "troll"), then you should immediately lower the priority.

- **Is it a troll?** Trolls are the bane of life on the Internet. Protected by the shroud of anonymity, trolls exist seemingly with the sole purpose of tearing things down. The best you can do is politely acknowledge their comments, and then do not engage them further. In Internet-speak, this advice is known as "Do not feed the trolls."

- **Be empathetic.** Make sure you figure out the commenter's emotional state. There's a difference between annoyed and genuinely angry, and your response must be tempered as best as possible to the person's emotions.

- **It's not a competition.** Recognize that you're not going to win over everyone or win every argument. In fact, put "win" out of your head right now. If you think of conversations as debates to be won or lost, you'll soon be in a downward spiral of he-said-she-said.

After your response (or non-response, as the case may be), keep an eye on the situation. Make sure that you're available for follow-up questions from the original complainant and any other people who might use the opportunity to chime in.

Customer Service

A very good use of social media channels is to utilize them as a direct customer service conduit to your customers. If you are a smaller company, this is an ideal way for customers to get their questions asked and answered.

That's because even though the phone and email still work, many customers are finding it more appealing and satisfying to complain in a more public forum, where not only the company will hear their complaints, but other people will as well. This gives the customer a sense of getting some real accountability from the organization, and any organization would do well to remember that to ignore such questions and comments would be foolish at best.

PayPal INSIDER

PayPal's Customer Service Channel

PayPal has learned that having a coordinated social media approach to customer support is very important to facilitating assistance to its customers.

Here at PayPal, social media has become so important to our customer service strategy that we created a separate AskPayPal Twitter account (http://twitter.com/ #!/ AskPayPal) manned by a full team of customer service representatives who respond directly to customer issues and questions.

Our Community Forums also give PayPal users the ability to deliver their questions about PayPal's products and services in a moderated forum environment where PayPal employees and fellow PayPal users can ask and answer each other's questions. There is even a scheduled weekly chat for users who want to ask their questions in a live format.

As part of your work in social media, you must be ready to monitor social media for such questions and answer them as promptly and completely as possible. This is not to say you have to drop everything to get to them, but it wouldn't be a bad idea to check in during lulls in your day. If you have a dedicated customer service team already, you should definitely assign resources to monitor social media channels and respond to questions.

Discounts

Finally, you might be thinking, here is some really targeted marketing—discounts. But there's a reason why this is the last one on the list; it should *not* be your highest priority.

Discounts and online coupons are nice for customers, but in social media terms they are like candy. They are really yummy to consume, but you cannot make a diet of them. You might get a number of friends and followers, but they won't be interested in your business, just whatever deal comes along next. That's not the kind of relationship you want to foster.

Discounts and any sort of ecoupon should be used in moderation. You can give them away randomly, or tie them to some fun contest, but they should be used sparingly. Too much "special" means that nothing is special at all.

The Last Word

Now that you've entered the conversation, you can start engaging with your audience and let them know what you and your organization are all about. It won't be a fast process, and success won't happen overnight, but with discipline and the right stuff, you'll be on your way to a successful social media presence.

But what is that right stuff? What's the secret sauce to a good social media campaign? As you'll see in Chapter 8, "Creating Content for Social Media," it's all about the content.

8

Creating Content for Social Media

It is one thing to be well versed in how to engage in conversation; it is quite another to be a good conversationalist.

The art of conversation is about having something meaningful to say. And what is true in face-to-face conversation is certainly true in social media. If you don't have something interesting to add to the conversation, then people will stop listening—and stop visiting your site.

The following tips will help you build better content for more engaging—and ultimately profitable— social media conversations.

Reading Minds

Approaching the subject of providing better content for a social media conversation is an easy thing to suggest, but how do you go about actually doing it?

One great way to figure out what to say is figuring out what your visitors want when they come to your company Web site, blog, or social media site. Doing this is easier than you might think, and you won't have to be a mind reader to do so.

When visitors come to your site, they usually show up by typing your website directly into the URL bar of their browser, following a link from another site, or running a search for some term in a search engine and finding content on your site that closely matches what they are looking for.

It is this last kind of entry into your site, known as an *organic search*, that will help you figure out what content is most interesting to your visitors now, and what will usually be interesting to them in the future.

Here's how this generally works. Let's say you have a typical website for your organization, a hardware store. Some time in the recent past, you decided to try to provide some helpful tips on how to do home maintenance. You wrote out some instructions, posted a few pictures to help illustrate the how-tos, and put them on your website.

Now, after some time, let's say you have a chance to look at the incoming traffic for individual pages on your site, and you notice that the traffic numbers for your clever method of replacing a screen on a window are significantly larger. Apparently, this is a very popular topic.

In fact, after further analysis, it turns out that this one Web page is among the top 10 sources of information for screen replacement, consistently placing at the top of search engines' first page of results for the term "screen replacement," and pretty high for "home repair." By happenstance, you've just walked into every Web marketer's dream: a natural hit.

So what do you do with it? If you're wise, you'll build on this and start adding similar content on your site, in the hopes that people who came for the first how-to might click around and see what other content gems you have.

This is search engine optimization (SEO) 101, which anyone with online marketing experience would be able to teach you. But the element of SEO that worked to boost your main website's traffic flow can also be of assistance in creating your social media conversations.

Most analytics tools, such as the free-of-charge Google Analytics, can provide insight into what's bringing your visitors into your business website. By tapping into your tool, such as the Matched Search Queries page, you can see what search terms people are using to find you.

TIP: There are a lot of SEO promises out there, some of which add up to empty promises that try to gimmick search engines with overtagging. Overtagging is the practice of flooding content with meta tags in the hopes of "gaming" a search engine into finding the content. The best SEO practice involves creating useful content, not tricks.

From such information, you should be able to find some topics that would interest incoming readers and get them to listen to you. This can also be applied to your social media content. If you note that a lot of people are coming to your site looking for information about a particular topic, then you can start framing social media conversations around that topic and related ones.

But beware: don't get tempted to stray too far from your core business. If you notice that a lot of people seem interested in a topic that's only vaguely related to your organization, don't let the tail wag the dog and change your business focus to match social needs. If your business needs to drastically shift its focus like that, then you will need a lot more data than some social media and Web analytics to make that call.

Another key point is not to place too much emphasis on this sort of research. While it can be useful to understand what potential audience members and customers are looking for, don't make these topics the sole focus of your social media content. Man, as it were, was not meant to live by window screening alone.

Building Content

Different social media outlets have different approaches to conveying information, so you need to provide content in specific ways. Let's take a look at the three text-based social media outlets—blogging, social network sites, and microblogging—and explore how to succeed in each one.

Blogging

Blogging is probably the most free-form social media outlet that you will have. Structured around the concept of a daily online journal, blogs have become one of the primary conduits of information on the Internet today.

Blogs are not just useful because they're easy to set up and maintain (though that's a big part of it). Blogs also have a lot of features that make them very social.

Most blogs have comments, where readers can chime in on your news and views, and you can respond back, so right away they can be the actual place where the conversation can happen and continue in subsequent blog entries.

Links to other content—especially other blogs—make up another useful tool. If you link to someone else's content, it is possible that eventually that person will see the inbound traffic coming in from your blog. If he is seeing a lot of traffic, he may see what you had to say, and perhaps start the discussion on a blog-to-blog level.

When you are thinking about content for your blog, here are some guidelines for blog writing:

- **Tell stories.** Everyone loves a good story. Stories have been used since we figured out language as a way to convey information to each other. If you want to learn about a new topic, you will be more interested if there are anecdotes or a narrative. Stories help us better relate to the author, and therefore to the content.

- **Teach.** When it comes to your organization, you need to be the expert at what you do. And because you are the expert, people will want to know what you know. So teach them. Whatever your expertise, be it writing, cheese-making, or project management, you have the opportunity to teach your readers about what it is you do and help them become more reliant on their own.

- **Inform.** If there's news happening about your organization, or even the broader industry, then you should break it, as journalists say. Don't make it all about your PR, either. If you're a food seller and there's an outbreak of E. coli, tell people about it from your perspective. What are you doing to protect them and your product? There's usually news—good and bad—about what your business does, so tell your customers so they're in the know about that, too.

- **Opine.** This one is tricky, but every once in a while, you're going to need to state your opinion on something affecting your business or the broader community. People will be looking to you for your opinion, and you'll need to deliver it. But above all else, you must be fair-minded as you try to persuade others to see your point of view. And never launch into a personal attack. Not only will you draw fire from the target of the attack, but you will also turn readers off as being overly combative.

Social Networks

A social network is any website that lets people build profiles and then connect those profiles to each other.

Using their profiles, participants can share information and items that are important to them, such as text, links to other sites, photos, and videos.

There are four major social network sites in the U.S.: Facebook, LinkedIn, Google Plus, and MySpace. Each site has its own culture, and as such, creating content on the site will have its unique challenges.

- **Facebook** is a robust and open platform for business. One of its most business-friendly features is Pages, which are essentially profiles for organizations instead of individual people.

  Business pages essentially function as self-contained blogs within the larger Facebook framework. But they have some much cooler features, such as the capability to add applications to a Page, which in turn can expand the experience for your Page's visitors.

- **LinkedIn** is a social network for professionals and a good place to communicate with your peers. Using connections within LinkedIn, you can reach out to fellow professionals and get direct information and share ideas in that manner.

- **MySpace** allows organizations to establish a presence within its network. Although there are no apps, you can blog within MySpace, so the blogging strategy listed earlier will still apply.

- **Google Plus** is a new social networking site in this list, relying on real-name profiles, which will help the network self-moderate. Based on the few commercial test accounts in the Google Plus network, it seems that Google Plus will offer profiles with the blog-like interface that other Google Plus users have. Content, therefore, can be tailored around the blogging model.

Other up and coming social network sites include the following:

- **Quora** is an online knowledge hub for mostly social media and technology questions. Ideally, Quora users ask questions about any particular topic, which are then answered by other users.

- **Dispora** is an open source site designed around the model that the users' data belongs to them.

PayPal INSIDER

PayPal and Facebook

PayPal's Facebook Page is designed to provide Facebook members with information about customer service, new products, and conferences. There's also access to exclusive deals found on our PayPal Shopping website.

The PayPal Page offers deals from our partners from PayPal Shopping, once a Facebook member chooses to Like the Page. These deals sometimes mirror those found at PayPal Shopping, but there are also exclusive-to-Facebook offers.

By offering this Page, PayPal not only provides Facebook users with valuable offers, but we also introduce them to important events and information about PayPal services.

One feature that is prevalent on all of these sites (except for LinkedIn) is the ability for users to add their own content to a profile. By either commenting directly on your content, or posting a public message to you (such as on Facebook's wall), this incoming content is a large part of what social media is all about. In Chapter 9, "Sharing with Rich Media," we'll discuss this type of rich content and explore how to encourage its use.

Microblogging

You may not have heard of "microblogging" before now, but it's the term used to describe social media sites that are limited to 140 characters or less. As such, whatever your content is, it will need to be very, very pithy.

While it may be hard to master the microblog form, after a while it will become second nature. But microblogs are less about content than about connections—if you send a message that's read by your followers, and a certain percentage of them resend that message to their followers (known as "retweeting" in Twitter-space), and so on, then suddenly you can reach hundreds of thousands of people with one message.

TIP: In April 2011, an Egyptian Cobra captured New York's attention when it escaped from the Bronx Zoo. @BronxZoosCobra soon captured 200,000 followers as it detailed the snake's "exploits" in the city, generating publicity for the Zoo and other mentioned businesses.

Don't expect that instant viral effect all the time. In fact, it's rare until you get a certain number of followers in a microblog network. That number is a bit indeterminate, but it's true that those with more followers are going to have a certain bit of cache and will be retweeted more often.

It is important to remember, though, that you don't want to use a microblog to just announce information about your business. Sure, you can point out your new blog entry, or a new sale, but also post things of interest: related news, topics that interest you and your customers, witty observations—all the things you would post in a regular blog, only much shorter.

Another good approach in a microblog service is reposting other people's entries. If you see something that interests you, then retweet it yourself. It's good manners, and there's a little "pay it forward" going on there, too.

You will want to use microblogging for conversations, more than broad-casting information. The whole format is an extension of cell-phone text-ing, so it's perfectly fine to have a Tweet be a public message to someone or many "someones." Get those two-way conversations going, and you'll find that a lot more interest will be generated toward what you have to say.

The Last Word

In this chapter, we reviewed the strategies needed to create and distribute really good social media content. These guidelines should give you a good place to start. The most important thing is to be disciplined. Don't adhere to a rigorous schedule, but don't wait three weeks between blog posts, either. Be consistent.

In Chapter 9, "Sharing with Rich Media," we'll examine how you can get content for your social media outlets that your users will provide. With photo and video sharing, suddenly you can collaborate on images and movies that will capture and hold audience attention for your business.

9

Sharing with Rich Media

The promise of social media lies in its very name: it's social in nature, which means there has to be some sort of interaction going on.

Thus far, we have examined how to produce content that others will enjoy, so they will hopefully follow your words and become interested in your organization. We have also encouraged a level of engagement from the audience, looking to start and continue online conversations.

But what if you could go further and actually encourage users to contribute new and original content of their own? This next step is what we'll review in this chapter.

Organic Content

Organic content refers to content that is contributed to a site by users, and not only is it a feature of social media sites, but it's also a prerequisite.

An easy example of organic content can be found on Wikipedia, where factual information is "crowdsourced," that is, contributed by anyone who believes he or she has knowledge to contribute, and peer-reviewed by anyone else reading the content.

All wikis benefit from the contributions of others. Indeed, they couldn't exist without user participation. You can even take that statement and apply it to every other social media platform.

Social media, it can easily be argued, has built a technology based solely on the contributions of user content. If users didn't provide their information, their updates, and their participation, there would be nothing upon which a social media platform could base itself.

On a practical level, this observation may not be so helpful. You're likely not thinking about launching your own social media platform. But the principle behind the social success of these networks can still apply to your organization: the most successful social ventures have some form of active community participation, something that should be nurtured.

There are several ways to encourage users to contribute content to your social media channels. Rich multimedia content, which has become very easy to produce these days, is an easy way to get participation, as well as a social media twist on a perennial favorite: the person-on-the-street interview.

Taking a Poll

If you want to get people's opinions, it's very easy to do: just ask them.

Here in the U.S., it seems, everyone has an opinion about, well, just about anything. If you want to attract attention, just start asking people what they think, and off they'll go. You can bring this to your social media channels easily by asking for your audience's opinions. If they're reading, they'll answer.

On a blog, asking questions can be as informal as simply ending your entry on a particular topic with a line like "What do you think?" or "What's your favorite/hated _____?"

You can also try something more formal. Blogging applications and services like WordPress, Tumblr, and Blogger have poll and survey tools available that can be plugged into your blog page, which will let your users respond to a "poll of the week" or other related questions, while allowing users to see the results and perhaps even comment on them.

Facebook also enables you to add questions right on your Facebook business page, just like adding any other kind of content. Here's how that's done:

1. On your business's Facebook page, click the Question link at the top of the Wall page. The Ask Something field will appear.

2. Enter your question in the Ask Something field.

3. Click the Add Poll Options link. The Poll Options fields will open.

4. Type the options for the question in the Add an Option fields. An option field will be added if you use all of the ones available.

5. If you want to make the question available to just a select group, click the Public button and select the Customize option in the drop-down control. The Choose Your Audience dialog will open.

6. Enter the appropriate information to establish the appropriate group. As you add options, new options will appear to further refine the choices.

7. Click Ask Question. The question will appear on your Wall.

Photos

Another way to create an interaction point with users is to invite them to submit photos to your company, while also publishing photos that are relevant to your organization.

Perhaps one of the best sites to accomplish this is to use the photo-sharing site Flickr, which lets your company not only upload photos and videos, but also any infographics you would care to share with your audience.

Since Flickr is a public photo-sharing site, you need to be careful of what you upload. Flickr is a useful resource for a lot of people and organizations, but as is true of many such sites, its community can be adverse to excessively commercial content. So if you think Flickr is going to be a good place to post your latest house ads, you'll be sorely mistaken. In fact, the Community Guidelines forbid outright selling practices.

Instead, try to follow these best practices for organizations, which Flickr itself recommends:

- Share interesting and original photos and videos. Don't make it about selling products. Make it about your history or your employees. Show those company picnic shots where Bob the CEO got nailed by that coconut cream pie. Or the disaster relief drive you organized for flood

Social Media SUCCESS STORY

C'est Cheese: The Fromage Beauty Pageant

Mari, having set up a blog account on WordPress, has been steadily blogging away for a couple of months, and seems to be getting a fair response on the traffic and comments. It's no Huffington Post, but the traffic numbers seem to indicate she's got a small and slowly growing core set of visitors. She would like to increase the amount of participation, and after noticing a vigorous discussion on posting pictures of finished recipes, she decides to open up a photo contest.

Setting it up was easy on Flickr. After creating a C'est Cheese Flickr group, she invited blog, Facebook, and Twitter followers (and her in-store customers) to send in their best-looking pictures of recipes using cheese, with the winners getting gift certificates to the store (and online catalog).

The rules were simple: contestants had to upload a photo of their best cheese-using recipe by a certain date to the C'est Cheese Flicker group. To keep things straight, she required photos to have the same tag: 2011RecipeContest.

After all was said and done, she had 47 entrants in the first contest. More importantly, by enabling comments on each Flickr photo, contestants and their viewers were exchanging comments and recipe tips on Flickr, which Mari was later able to compile into a Winners' Showcase post on Facebook and the blog.

Though the contest was a success, Mari has decided that next year she will need to print out instructions on how to upload photos to Flicker properly, as some of her customers were unable to participate because they couldn't sort out how to use Flickr.

victims. As Flickr says, "Flickr is for photosharing—so use your account to share photos, not to sell things."

- Create a transparent and authentic identity. Don't put the company up as your face—be the face of the company.

Flickr is a great site for storing and displaying such imagery, as long as you abide by these rules. Flickr uses a "freemium" model, where photos and video storage is free up to a point, after which Flickr charges a nominal amount for their pro account with unlimited storage.

Posting a photo on Flickr is simple, as you can see in the following steps:

1. In Flickr, click the You menu and select the Upload Photos and Videos option. The Upload to Flickr page will appear.

2. Click the Choose Photos and Videos link. The Select Files dialog will open.

3. Navigate to the file(s) you want to upload and select them to upload.

4. Click Open. The files will be listed.

5. Click the appropriate privacy options.

6. Click Upload Photos and Videos. The files will be uploaded, notifying you with a Finished message when complete.

7. Click the Add a Description link. The Describe This Upload page will appear.

8. Add descriptions and tags to the images as needed. When complete, click Save at the bottom of the page. The images will be displayed in your account's photostream page.

Tagging photos is the practice of assigning one or more categories to images, be it in your private collection on your computer or online in a social media platform like Flickr or Facebook. A "tag" can be assigned to one or more photos, and it enables you (or someone else) to find photos based on semantic searches. So, instead of renaming every photo from last Summer "SummerVacation_001.jpg,"

CAUTION: Take care when tagging photos of people, as not all social media contacts will want their image tagged enabling it to be found easily.

"SummerVacation_002.jpg," and so on, you can leave the filenames for the image alone and just assign a "Summer Vacation" tag. Tags can describe context, people, locations—anything you want.

Video

Video is another area where you can start a discussion and also start collecting organic content.

Thanks to sites like YouTube and Vimeo, uploading a video is very easy, making sharing this sort of content a very painless process.

NOTE: Vimeo is a video site much like YouTube, with its own advantage: users can submit videos longer than 10 minutes.

Like Flickr and other social media sites, blatant commercial activity is not welcome on these video-sharing sites. The only exception seems to be the annual Super Bowl commercials and the occasional entertaining commercial that pops up during the year.

That doesn't preclude you from getting your message out there. One of the best ways to utilize your profile on one of these services (referred to on YouTube, for instance, as a *channel*) is to record and upload informative videos, particularly how-to content. Your customers, and indeed the entire Internet, will appreciate useful information.

PayPal INSIDER

Lights, Camera, PayPal

PayPal's YouTube Channel is primarily used to demonstrate the various features of our products and services. Our videos show PayPal how-tos, so of course the info mainly interests select merchants more than a majority of YouTube visitors, but our Near-Field Communications solution video, which briefly highlights how NFC-equipped devices can be used to transmit funds directly from one party to another, is highly popular.

By showing visual demonstrations of our products, we can keep customers up-to-date with our latest services and their potential to impact lives.

Video sites also lend themselves well to organic content. You can encourage users to upload video responses to your content, participate in video content, or post reviews of your business. Because of the instant narrative found in videos, users may actually prefer them to other forms of content, as some people can be more verbally oriented.

On YouTube, uploading a video is a snap:

1. In YouTube, click the Upload link at the top of the page. The Video File Upload page will appear.

2. Click the Upload Video button. A File Open dialog will appear.

3. Navigate to the video you want to upload and click Open. The video will be uploaded to the YouTube site.

4. Fill in the Title, Description, and Tags fields.

5. Select a Category for the video.

6. Set the Privacy and License options for the video.

7. Click Save Changes. The video will be posted to YouTube.

The Last Word

You have seen a few examples of how social media can be enhanced using multimedia content, as well as encouraging organic content provided by your own audience. Such methods are very useful for building the level of participation in your own social media channels.

In Chapter 10, "Using Promotions to Generate More Sales," we'll demonstrate how social media can be used in coordinated efforts to increase donations for your non-profit organization and sales for your commercial venture.

Part 4

MONETIZING SOCIAL MEDIA WITH PAYPAL

10

Using Promotions to Generate More Sales

Throughout this book, we have emphasized the idea that social media is all about the conversation. If you create a conversation with your customers, they will become more engaged with you and your organization, and your organization will prosper from the healthier relationship.

That is certainly true, and it represents the critical idea to remember about social media and business: it's a process that takes time to build. Of course, there also will be times when you'll want to promote something important—a new product, a sale, a fund drive—in a short-term timeframe. When that happens, social media can be used as a marketing tool to help build participation in your promotion, no matter what it is.

Make the Plan

Like building your long-term social media community, creating a promotion typically can't be done on the fly. Nor should it. Even if you are a marketing expert who intuitively "gets" how to run a promotion from start to finish, you'll still want to make a plan, for two very important reasons.

First, there's accountability. If your work is being judged by others, then you will need to provide a framework upon which those people (perhaps your supervisors) can base their criteria.

Second, there's the issue of legacy. In software development circles, this is often known as the "What if so-and-so quits?" problem. It sounds rather painful, but in actuality it addresses the very important issue of what happens when a software developer moves on from a particular project. Who will take over for him and has he left behind the right sort of information to allow that new person to take his place?

It's not just a software development problem—legacy is a problem for everyone. If you are promoted, or transferred, or otherwise leave, who will take over for you and how will your replacement do the work?

That's why it's important to have a plan—even if you're a marketing expert.

For the rest of us, you need a plan for your social media promotion for a third, and very critical reason: without a plan, your social media promotion will likely be unsuccessful. You don't need to script every single detail, but you need to work out the major details of your promotion, because you don't want inconsistencies making your audience upset.

Do the Research

Before you do your promotion, you need to get online and see if anyone has done something similar.

Don't worry if your idea isn't original; unless a direct competitor has run the same promotion, it should not stop you from trying something similar. If a competitor has already tried your idea, don't be discouraged. You can learn what worked or didn't work in his implementation.

The key is, if you have an idea for a promotion, find a similar promotion and learn from it—it's like finding a pot of gold. You can read online how the promotion unfolded. What worked for the organization? What didn't? If you don't find the details you want online, you should be able to find contact information about the organization and ask them directly how the promotion worked. If you're polite, you can ask them about more details on the business side of the promotion.

If you're having trouble locating organizations willing to discuss their social media campaigns, try joining a specific marketing social media community, such as the one found at The CMO Site (www.thecmosite.com), which discusses promotional ideas that have worked or didn't work and why.

TIP: If you do get detailed information on another organization's promotion, offer to share the results of your promotion when it's finished. That way, you both can learn from each other's experiences.

Create an Outline

Once you have researched promotions that are similar to what you want to do, you need to create an outline citing how your promotion is going to go.

It is very important to understand that you will not be creating a step-by-step script of every single step in your promotion. There's no need to put in that kind of work, because you are bound to have some unexpected developments that would throw you off the script. Instead, the outline serves to list the major points of your promotion. At a bare minimum, it should include (but not be limited to) the following information:

- The type of promotion
- The theme of the promotion
- The social media channels to be used
- The participants in the promotion
- The responsibilities of each participant

- The materials needed for the promotion

- The goals of the promotion

That's the minimum, mind you—you may also want to construct a loose timeline of the sequence of events of the promotion. But if you have at least these minimum pieces of knowledge worked out, you will be able to stay on track with the promotion, no matter what happens.

Set the Goals

Keen observers will have noted the last required point on the outline: the goals of the promotion. Often, promotions will be launched with just vague goals in mind: "get more people in the store" or "successfully launch new company."

Instead, it's important to set concrete, measureable goals for the promotion so that you can see how it truly performed. Did it adequately meet your expectations, or better, did it knock those expectations out of the park? If the promotion didn't work out as planned, analyze the results after it's all said and done for insights into what went wrong and what went right.

The types of goals that can be measured in a promotional campaign include the following:

- **Increased sales/donations.** This is the first-level goal for most organizations—a specific increase in the sale of a particular item or the amount of donations received.

- **Awareness.** This is a more loosely defined goal but valid nonetheless. It involves making your organization more prominent in your social community. Specific metrics would include attendance at a specific event or an increase in the number of new contacts on an organizational mailing list.

- **Participation.** This goal may revolve around a specialized major event, where you need people to participate for the event to succeed. This could include a community fundraising event in which your organization is participating.

Choose the Type of Promotion

As you might imagine, there are many different kinds of promotions you can try. Just look at the early days of television for, shall we say, creative examples of promotions, where the dignified salesman of used cars would climb into a chicken suit to entice his customers to come on down for great deals.

But unlike the chicken suits of yore, your promotions can be fun and productive at the same time. You just have to know your audience and figure out what will work best for them.

Hold a Contest

The idea of a social media contest is pretty simple. Essentially, you will post information about the contest on a social network or microblogging site and ask your audience to share that information with their friends or followers.

Pre-social media examples of such contests might be Kodak's photography contests, where contestants could compete for prizes by submitting photos on various subjects. And while Kodak has changed from its days of film and paper, the contests still go on.

In a social media setting, people can be entered into the contest by either a quick registration on a website or social network page, or even by simply sharing the information about the contest. This is the easiest way to get people involved in your contest. For example, on Twitter you could ask followers to retweet a link to your website or mention your Twitter handle (such as @AskPayPal), company name, or product to be automatically entered in your contest. Or you could ask people on Facebook to "like" your contest page on that social network to be entered to win. It's very much up to you.

TIP: When someone clicks "Like" on Facebook for a company or product, the person's Facebook wall could be inundated with events and news about that company. This could be quite irritating to Facebook users, so be sure your promotional page keeps such content to a minimum.

Keep your goals in mind, though, as you think about how the contest will run. If you're trying to increase the notoriety of your Facebook presence, then make sure that your brand appears in the contest name when sending requests to Facebook users to enter the contest. When they re-share the information with their friends, then your brand will get carried along for the ride.

Or, if you want to gather customer information, then you will want to bring in the users to a Web page where they'll need to enter their information on a small form.

> **TIP:** A "small" entry form is the operative word: don't make your contest participants have to enter a lot of information. Keep it simple, requiring only basic contact information, like name, email, and address (for identity purposes).

Here are some other considerations when developing a contest:

- **Know the law of the land.** Contests can have different federal and state laws governing them, depending on where your organization is based. Ever see those disclaimers on a contest that say "Not valid for residents of such-and-such state"? That's because such-and-such state may have legislation that prevents certain contests from being run. Contact your local or state attorney's office to find out exactly what you can and can't do. If you're giving away a valuable item or services, you may want to consult an attorney to go over your rules to make sure you haven't missed anything.

- **Come up with a cool prize.** Maybe your business has such interesting and desired services or products that coming up with a prize will be a no-brainer. But if you don't, try to be creative in what you give away. If you own a car dealership, you may not be able to afford to give away a car, but you could offer free oil changes for a year, for instance.

- **Create a landing page.** Even if you don't require much input from entrants for contest participation, you will need to set up a landing page for entrants to visit. This page will have the details for the contest, with the complete rules and how the prizes will be awarded. You won't want any ambiguity to upset the contest, so this page is important.

- **Stay with the contest.** Track how your contest is going. If your contest is based on work submitted, such as with a photo or video contest, highlight entrants on a daily or weekly basis. This will generate more interest from that specific entrant and the contest as a whole.

Contests are a fun way to promote your business, and social media is tailor-made to run them without a lot of costs. Just make sure you have everything detailed and spelled out, to ensure your contest is legitimate for everyone. Your sense of fun will be picked up by the entrants and keep the contest more enjoyable for them.

Host a Real-World Event

If you have a brick-and-mortar business, you can pull in people to your location with a special real-world event.

Such events are not hard to organize: schedule a date and time (perhaps after normal business hours) and bring people in for a special just-for-social-media-fans event. It could be a sale. Or a special product debut. It could even be a civic-oriented meeting that addresses an issue in your community.

The type of event is not terribly critical—it doesn't even have to be a direct sales opportunity. You want people to come into your business, get to know you and your staff, and feel comfortable about your business. You can also use this as an opportunity to give local social media users a chance to meet each other face-to-face, which is usually a nice change for them after all those online conversations.

Log on to an Online Event

Online events are becoming more and more common these days. These coordinated gatherings on the Internet can range from something as simple as a Google Plus gathering, where participants can jump onto a video conference call at a certain time and date, to a full-fledged multi-day training seminar.

Obviously, the bigger the scale of your event, the more complex it is to plan. If you want to start with something simple, try one of these ideas:

- **Run a Twitter Chat.** Twitter (or any microblog) chats are a great way to get customer feedback or set yourself up as a knowledgeable source for your products or business. Using a special hashtag, get your audience into a broader conversation about the topic of the week or month. Chances are followers will start sharing the conversations and chime in themselves.

- **Host a Social Network Event.** You can also hold a robust chat session on a social network like Facebook or Dispora. Simply set up an event page and then invite all your guests to jump on the page at a specific time. You can encourage them to bring their friends, if they feel the conversation's getting interesting.

Online events like these are not especially tricky to set up from a technical standpoint. In fact, many social media networks make it easy to implement social events like these online. The real trick is, like in any social gathering, keeping the conversation fresh, interesting,

Social Media SUCCESS STORY

C'est Cheese: Not Just for Storefronts

Mari has been working with local dairies for years, highlighting their products in various promotions and sales. There's a lot of good cheese out there, after all, and some of it's just down the road.

Mari has brought her customers to the store for various events organized online—the monthly wine and cheese events are especially popular. But now Mari wants to try something else: working with one of the larger local farms, she organizes a field trip to the farm, located about an hour out of town.

Splitting the cost of transportation, a chartered bus, with the dairy, Mari soon has a busload of her customers and a couple of her staff on the farm where this local cheese is made. The farm

operators and owners fete the customers with a pleasant weekend afternoon of watching cheese production, hand-milking cows, and sampling the farm's wares (with a little wine, of course).

The customers come away with a much greater appreciation of how cheese is made, and there are a few converted fanatics for this particular farm's cheese, too. Even the staff members that went along on the tour start selling that brand of cheese a little more, telling customers their first-hand experiences about the cheese that they just watched getting made and aged.

It's a big win for Mari and the local farmer, and they're already planning another trip.

and as much on-target as you can. Sometimes the conversation will go off-topic, and that's okay. But if you have a specific point to make, you will want to steer the discussion back to your topic every once in a while.

Measure Your Results

The final task that you should be undertaking with your promotion, no matter what it turns out to be, is measuring the results of the event. How many people entered your contest or showed up at your real or virtual event?

More importantly, how did the social media tools work for you? What were the re-sharing rates on the social media platforms you used? How many visits did your landing page get?

Analyze these numbers carefully, using the techniques and analysis that will be discussed in Chapter 11, "Evaluating Your Social Media Success," because you will want to know what worked and what didn't work in your promotion. After all, if you're going to do it again, you'll want to do it better the next time.

The Last Word

In this chapter, we examined how you can use social media to build and manage successful promotions, and we looked at some examples of the kinds of promotions that work.

Any of these promotions discussed can add real value to your business, for the direct effect of increasing your revenue, as well as for the value of strengthening the connection between your organization and its customers.

In Chapter 11, "Evaluating Your Social Media Success," you'll learn how to discover the true impact of your social media efforts and how to apply metric analysis into improving your social media growth. Such metrics will also help merchants make more social media related sales and non-profits more revenue.

11

Evaluating Your Social Media Success

Throughout this book, social media has been framed as a conversation. And while that is most certainly a good description, at a certain point there will be a need to analyze these conversations and figure out just how they are affecting your business.

At the end of the day, you are going to need to quantitatively measure what you are doing and figure out if it's helping you drive sales to your business, memberships and donations to your organization, or whatever you are trying to accomplish.

An Introduction to Metrics

Metrics are a funny thing. On the one hand, they seem pretty simple to understand, and yet they are the most misunderstood aspect of business analysis.

Here's the simple definition: metrics represent the value of something you measure. Let's say you measure your TV, and it's 52 inches wide. That's a decent-sized screen by most people's definition. But that word "value" has a straightforward mathematical definition that's objective, such that "52 inches" is empirical, as well as subjective, as in the subjective value we place on something; to you, that television might represent hours of work to save the money to buy it.

Here's another, less materialistic example that may help drive the point home. Your child or grandchild is (empirically) 52 inches tall. But the child's value to you is beyond measure.

This is the real trick with metrics, something that we have struggled with throughout history. It's only become much more heightened in the age of the Internet because we're trying to measure said Internet, while at the same time using that same Internet to discuss better ways to handle metrics.

Call it a positive feedback loop.

As time has gone by, some Internet metrics have evolved that have become very useful. For instance, in the early days of the Web, the key information to track was how many visitors you had coming to your site. That was easy: just count the number of times your home page was served.

But the increase of commercial advertising on the Web soon created a demand for more metrics. How many of those visitors were unique and not repeating customers? (Answer: start counting IP addresses.) But then you needed to know how long visitors were staying on your site. Were they just coming in, looking around, and leaving? Or were they sticking around and checking out all the other content on your site? (Answer: start measuring the amount of time spent on your site.)

And so on.

Many of the metrics developed for website analysis can be (and have been) applied to social media, but since social media is such a nascent field, there's some uncertainty as to what measurements should be given value.

Number of friends and followers is something that one would expect to be given value, but is it really a pure measurement? Say someone has 5,000 followers on Twitter, for instance, and asks followers to send in $20 to a particular charity. If 100 followers comply, then $2,000 is raised, and we can say this person has an active reach—in this example, of 2 percent.

Now, let's say another person makes the same call for donations, and he only has 500 followers, but it's a much tighter group of like-minded individuals, and 50 people send in their donations. In this second example, only $1,000 is raised, but the Twitter network has an active reach of 10 percent, which is much higher.

Looking at each of these examples, it's difficult to say how much weight should be put on the raw number of Twitter followers. On the one hand, the second person with the smaller network seems to have a more effective reach. But it's also hard to ignore that because of the size of the first Twitterer's network, she was able to create more action overall.

You can see where the uncertainty comes in. For the remainder of this chapter, we'll lay out the different types of metrics that we believe are useful for a business to track, how to track these measurements, and some examples of how to build some overall analytical plans.

Social Network Metrics

There are quite a few different forms of social media metrics that you can begin tracking right away. Some of them translate directly from Web media because they assume that social media will be used as a channel to drive traffic to your website, where presumably sales will be made on your ecommerce system.

Even if you don't sell products and services on the Web, you can use these metrics, because you can still track in-bound traffic to your business by monitoring how many people send you emails based on your social activity or how many fill out the "contact us" form on your website.

Here are the metrics you can use and the tools to measure them.

Leads

Like any other form of marketing, you'll want to track your leads as they come in from the social media platforms.

This should be a two-stage approach. First, you need to track traffic as it comes into your site so you know which social media platforms are the most active. This can be done with any standard analytics tool, such as Google Analytics.

In parallel to gathering this kind of information, you also need to capture potential client information as it comes in. As you continue the conversation with clients, you should also be collecting basic contact details, such as Facebook names, Twitter handles, and so on. This information should then be entered into a Customer Relation Management (CRM) tool, so your sales and marketing staff can use the information to follow up later with these same customers.

Care should be taken as to how you handle this; if you treat every contact as a potential customer, you'll end up sending them spam. It's better to instruct your sales and marketing teams to back off until the staff member handling social media feels confident that the person on the other end of the conversation would welcome a chat with them. Even better: train your social media team to refrain from sending the information to sales and marketing until it's appropriate, thus preventing any jumping of the gun.

Knowing what's an appropriate time is always a hard thing to gauge; here are some ideas:

- Pass the lead to the sales team if the person explicitly asks for such a contact.

- Ask them in a low-key way when they think they might be ready to discuss their needs with your sales team.

- Above all else, keep it low-pressure; it's a conversation, not a full-on sales pitch.

CRM tools will help automate all activities related to customer relationship management. You'll find a number of really good CRM tools out there, such as SugarCRM, an open source CRM system that has a lot of features at a reasonable cost. Or if you want a CRM system that's more automated and integrated with your social media systems, you might want to look at HubSpot, a product that does a very good job of handling inbound marketing on the social network level.

Bounces

Bounces, or *bounce rate*, is data that comes straight out of Internet metrics. Remember earlier in this chapter, when we discussed the metric for measuring how many visitors came to your site's pages. That was bounce rate.

Specifically, bounce rate is the percentage of single-page visits that people make to your website, versus coming on and looking around at other pages in the site. Generally, the lower the bounce rate percentage, the more interested they are in your site.

Since social media landing pages are always single-page, bounce rate can't strictly apply to your actual social media pages. But you can apply bounce rate to social media by examining bounce rate statistics for visitors coming in from social media links. In that way, you can see if your social media efforts are encouraging those visitors to be more engaged with your Internet presence.

Tracking social media bounce rates can be done with any good analytics tool. All you have to do is tune your bounce rate filters to look at incoming traffic from social media links.

Size

Earlier in the chapter, the discussion was focused on whether or not the size of a social network was actually the most important factor in determining social media success.

While that question is murky, there is no doubt that the size of a network has some bearing on your social media implementation, so it's best to track this.

More important than the actual size, you should track the rate of change in your networks. If the rate new members are joining is increasing with time, you are doing well. Conversely, a slowdown of growth or even a full reversal of your social media network's growth can indicate a problem with your social media strategy.

Keeping this metric is easy—just look at your network size on a weekly basis and track it in your favorite database or spreadsheet application. Then you can graph it to see the rate of change.

Mentions

It's not just how many of your network members you communicate with; it's also how many of them turn around and mention your company or product. Or how many share something you've posted on your own social media channel.

This is really about two distinct measurements. First, there's the traditional brand mention aspect, which anyone in marketing will want to track. Knowing how often your company, product, or brand is getting mentioned is important to evaluating your overall marketing impact.

There's more to this than just mentioning your business; you will also need to know how your brand is being mentioned. Is it positive or negative? Is it trending up or down? Social media monitoring services like Brandwatch can keep an eye on this for you, for a fee, or you can set up a search filter in a tool like TweetDeck or HootSuite to monitor mentions and even related industry terms.

PayPal INSIDER

🏠 Sharing Our Blog

On our official PayPal blog (www.thepaypalblog.com), each blog entry has a TweetThis plug-in widget, which lets readers retweet a link to the blog if they would like to share it.

We also recommend tracking the number of times that readers click on outbound links. When readers click on links in your content, it suggests they trust your opinion and suggestions. This is a great measure of influence and brand loyalty.

Blogs

Blogs fall into a unique position within social media metrics, because they are social media platforms in and of themselves, as well as great generators of social media conversations.

For the pure blog part of the equation, the standard metrics will apply. But you'll also need to track comments in the blog itself, as well as any Twitter or Facebook mentions that might be made about the blog entry.

In order to get social media stats about your blog, it's a good idea to include tools in the blog that will enable users to share your content on their social media networks. All of the major blog platforms (Blogger, WordPress, Drupal, and Joomla!) have plug-ins that easily enable such sharing.

Analyzing Your Data

There is a lot of social media data that you can gather for your business, but gathering data alone is not enough. You have to be able to apply that data to measuring the achievement of specific goals.

And by specific, we mean it. You could say, for example, that you want to increase your social media influence by a certain amount (say twice as much), but that goal, while technically measureable, is rather hard to pin down due to its generality.

It's better instead to create a specific, measureable goal, such as "increase blog traffic by 20 percent in three months' time" or "on Facebook get X percent more fans in a certain amount of time."

Beyond the goals of increasing social media influence and footprint for its own sake, you will also want to analyze data in relation to actual business costs.

For example, if you plan to use social media to supplement your existing customer service channel, you will want to pull together data in such a way that tracks how much time (and money) your company is putting into each customer service request. If you have real, hard data like this, you can compare it to your other customer service channels and see how effective social media is.

Conversions

Of course, all the social activity in the world won't make a lot of difference if it doesn't lead to more sales or other measurable participation in your organization.

This conversion from marketing to actual activity (sales, donations, volunteers, and so on) is known as *conversion*. As you generate leads from marketing, the better your conversion of those leads, the better your revenue stream will be (if you're a for-profit business).

Sometimes, in social media circles, conversion will also be used synonymously with return on investment (ROI). While they are similar, they are not the same thing. ROI is just one way of measuring conversion. Another way would be the number of donations that arise from a marketing campaign. ROI has the advantage of being a more measureable figure, though, since you can plug in what you spent on the marketing campaign and then measure the end results and get the ROI figure.

There is a lot of evidence that suggests that because social media conversations are inherently more personable than other online marketing efforts, such as organic search optimization or paid search ads, then the quality of your leads will be better right from the get-go.

The reasoning behind this line of thought is that social media, unlike other, less connected ways of reaching potential customers, can communicate the intent of your leads far more effectively than in those other communication channels. It's a quantity versus quality argument: sure, a paid search engine ad campaign might generate more leads by virtue of the fact that more eyeballs have seen the ad, but will the conversion rate be as high as a smaller-scale set of conversations between real people with potential interest in your business?

Social media, it should be noted, is only the first part of the conversion process. If you are genuine in your conversations and producing high-quality content, then more people will ultimately come into your site or store. In marketing lingo, you've raised the customer to the top of the funnel. At the bottom of the funnel is your objective—the action you want these potential customers to do.

But now you have to get them to the other end of the funnel. In a storefront operation, that means making them feel welcome and genuinely assisted, and it is here that all the rules about great customer service apply.

In an online environment, you should take steps to make sure that incoming social media leads feel welcome as well. Make a special landing page for them that acknowledges where they came from ("Welcome Facebook Users!"). If you had a theme going in your social media conversation, make sure that theme continues on your website.

Also, be very clear on the landing page what you want your potential customers to do. If it's making a donation, have the donation button right there on the landing page—don't make them drill down three or four pages to the donation page.

PayPal is also another tool that can help you with your conversions, by virtue of the fact that PayPal's products can create sales through managing efficient and successful transactions.

The Last Word

Measuring the true impact of your social media activity is not going to be a simple matter of tracking one or two statistics and then calling it done. You will need to compile different sets of data and use them in combination to determine the intent of your audience and how you can enhance the conversation as well as achieve your business goals.

In Chapter 12, "Integrating PayPal with Websites," we'll look at how to create a more streamlined sales or donation channel for your organization using PayPal ecommerce and payment tools.

12

Integrating PayPal with Websites

As you explore how to connect to customers using social media, you may be looking for opportunities to streamline your existing ecommerce site. It stands to reason, after all, that the easier you can make final sales happen, the better your conversion rate will be.

This is where the use of PayPal tools can really come in handy. Using PayPal as an ecommerce payment tool in conjunction with a social media strategy can be a real asset to your organization.

In this chapter, then, we'll learn how to connect various PayPal tools to your ecommerce site, either from scratch or by using third-party tools.

Choosing an Integration Path

Since there are many PayPal products out there, you'll find more than one option to integrate PayPal into your website.

By integration, we mean inserting some sort of code into the underlying code of your existing website so that PayPal functionality will be provided. For example, some code inserts the buttons and links necessary for your customers to purchase items and access the customer's shopping cart and checkout system. Other code links information on your site and input by your customers to functionality hosted by PayPal. Still other code generates forms to accept customer information or even checkout pages. The code that's inserted depends on, naturally, which PayPal product you want to use.

At this point, you may be wondering what you've signed up for, particularly if you're not a developer or website manager. Don't sweat it—explaining these technical details is helpful for those who are developers, but even if you're not a developer, it's also useful to give you an idea of the functionality each tool will have.

HTML Integration

The first and easiest type of PayPal integration involves the use of blocks of HTML code.

HTML is the language of the Web. It underlies virtually every site on the Internet, presenting information that browsers can interpret and display in creative ways.

If you are already familiar with HTML coding, then this form of integration will be a snap. Even better, PayPal has tools that will actually generate the code you need, making it ready to insert into your site.

HTML integration is appropriate for these two PayPal products:

- **Website Payments Standard**. PayPal services are integrated with your website or ecommerce application via HTML code by creating payment buttons using PayPal's button creation tool. You can create Buy Now, Add to Cart, View Cart, Subscribe, and Donate buttons that link to the proprietary PayPal Shopping Cart. You can also use HTML code to link these buttons to third-party shopping carts and checkout systems. This option is typically used by smaller businesses.

- **Payflow Link**. This HTML-based product provides a gateway page hosted by PayPal that acts as a go-between from your shopping cart to your merchant services account. These PayPal-hosted pages are fully customizable and can be made to match the look and feel of your website.

Using an HTML integration method is a set-and-forget type of activity. After the PayPal site generates the HTML code for the elements you need, you just insert that code into the appropriate Web pages and off you go.

The reason these HTML-based solutions are simple to implement is because all the back-end operations take place on the PayPal site. Your site doesn't actually host the shopping cart or checkout system, so you don't have to create shopping cart and checkout pages. Instead, clicking a Purchase or Payment button takes your customers to PayPal's site, where all the safe transactions take place. Afterwards, customers are returned to your site (see **Figure 12.1**).

Because of the simplicity of the back-end operations in an HTML-based tool, these solutions work very well for small businesses that have fewer items to sell. Such businesspeople can easily create a page on their websites that sells a few things and add a PayPal payment button for a single item or each item on the sale page. After it's set, PayPal will handle

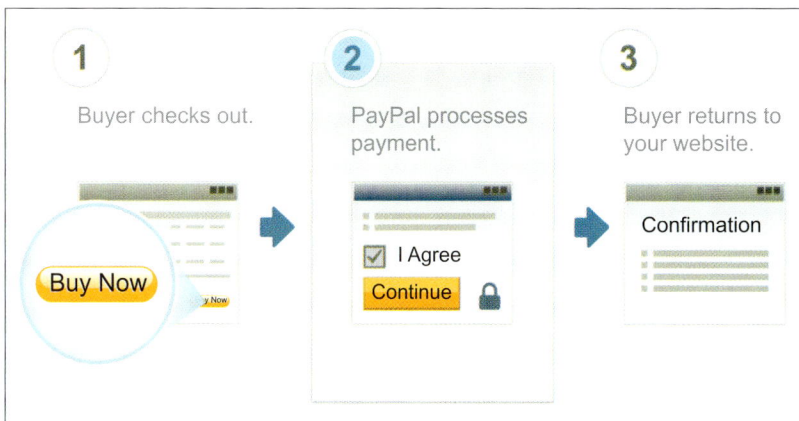

Figure 12.1
PayPal's HTML-based checkout process directs customers to PayPal's site and back again.

all subsequent orders and notify you when there's been a purchase and by whom so you can ship the product.

The transaction can be made to look as seamless as possible for customers, so that they may not even notice the departure from your site, which they temporarily leave to complete the transaction. And even if they can tell, it should not affect your sales negatively, since PayPal is one of the most trusted sites.

But, if you have a lot of inventory for sale that isn't static, then you'll want to consider a better option: API integration.

API Integration

If you are a larger business or someone who has a lot of items to sell, you may not want to use HTML integration and PayPal's hosted checkout services. In this case, you will need to use what's known as API integration to connect your products with PayPal.

APIs link data from your website to the PayPal system. This is done in real time, thus providing a constant connection between your site and PayPal's site. The benefit here is that when you make any changes to your online catalog, PayPal will be informed at checkout, and you won't have to keep creating new Buy Now buttons with the new information.

PayPal INSIDER

HTML Integration, the Best Option for Smaller Sellers

If you're a small business or an individual offering only a few products for sale online, we recommend PayPal's Website Payments Standard. It's easy to add a payment button to your website or blog by inserting a few lines of HTML code: PayPal handles the shopping cart and checkout processing. There's no need to build or buy your own shopping cart or checkout system.

Also, HTML integration provides a huge benefit to small to medium businesses, as they get automatic Payment Card Industry (PCI) compliance. Because these business sites don't access sensitive financial data (it's all handled by us at PayPal), they don't have to secure their transaction website.

As you can see in **Figure 12.2**, PayPal's API-based solutions lead your customers on your website throughout the checkout process; the APIs communicate with PayPal to obtain necessary information or perform required functions.

NOTE: API stands for Application Programming Interface, a set of rules or specifications that can access and use services from another website or application. APIs are like the glue that holds different Web applications together.

As the figure shows, PayPal still handles the payment processing, but now it sends the resulting information back to either your site or the third-party checkout system that you might be using to wrap up the process.

If are hosting your own ecommerce pages, such as a shopping cart and checkout pages, the API integration is more involved than simply inserting a few lines of HTML code into a Web page. Would that it were that simple. What has to happen now is that API functions need to be incorporated within the code or script responsible for getting information from the customer, sending that information to PayPal, calling the appropriate PayPal function, and then returning the processing information back to your website for display to the customer.

Yeah, not so simple. This is pretty much why API programming is not for the technically inexperienced. You'll need a qualified developer to do the appropriate programming on your website. But the payoff should be worth it: seamless PayPal integration with your existing ecommerce site.

Here are the PayPal products that utilize API integration:

- **Website Payments Pro**. All-in-one payment solution that functions as both a merchant account and a payment gateway.

- **Payflow Pro**. Uses PayPal APIs to provide a payment gateway between your existing merchant credit card account and PayPal so that you can process credit card transactions online.

- **Express Checkout**. Used with another PayPal service (such as Website Payments Pro and Payflow Pro) and gives users with PayPal accounts a streamlined experience with fewer and shorter steps.

Figure 12.2
PayPal's API-based checkout process transfers customer and product data to PayPal and back again.

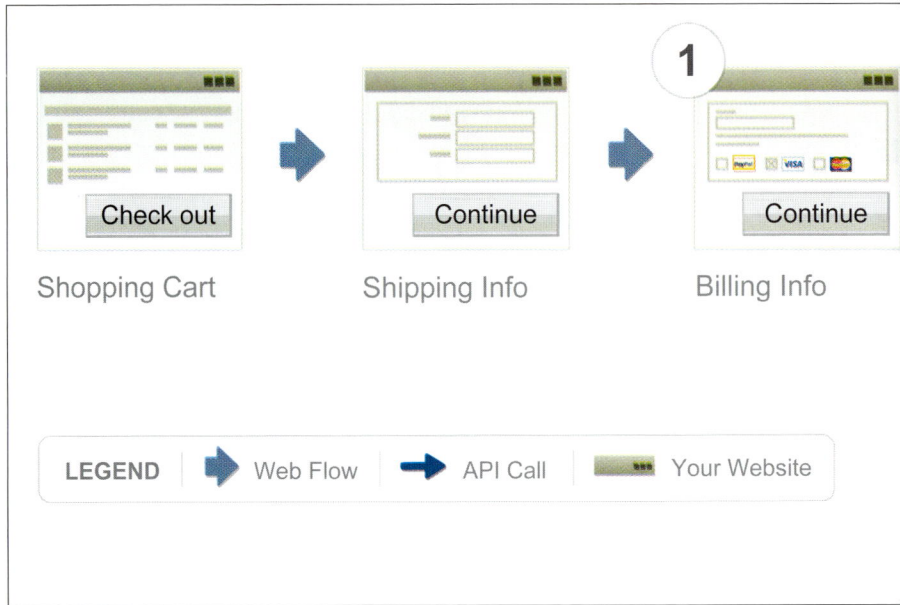

ADVANTAGES OF API INTEGRATION

HTML integration is all well and good for smaller retailers with just a few items to sell, or a larger business with more items but an inventory that changes infrequently.

But if this is not the case for you, then adding and maintaining all those HTML-coded buttons could be a real pain to keep up. There are also good reasons for not wanting your customers to go off-site in the checkout process. As good as PayPal's checkout system is, it's not your site, with all of the branding and potential conversion links your site could have.

Keeping customers on-site will help make their experience on your site a seamless one, which is always a better plan.

Using PayPal's API-based options, you or a Web developer will need to do a bit more programming, since you will have to build your own checkout pages or integrate a third-party shopping cart solution.

PayPal's API solutions cost no more than the HTML solutions, as far as charges from PayPal go. There are still the usual transaction fees, but like HTML integration, it costs nothing to plug into PayPal's services. The extra

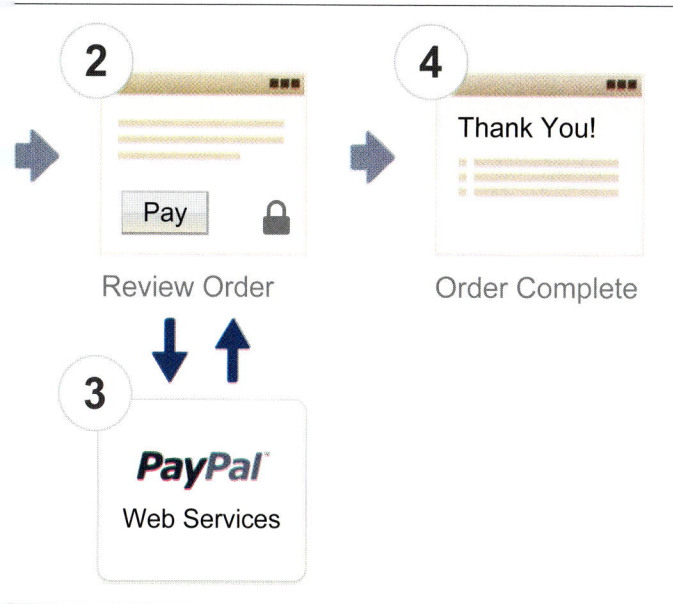

costs will be incurred in the resources and time it takes you to develop your own ecommerce pages, but if you are using the API services, you were likely going to pay those costs anyway. What will definitely be an extra charge is the amount of time and effort needed to integrate PayPal's API services with your site, so you will need to take this into account.

If you're running a large ecommerce site, then you know you will want a branded checkout solution; the risk of losing an opportunity to convert more sales may be too high by sending customers off site.

THIRD-PARTY SHOPPING CARTS

There is one good way to minimize the effort of API integration: use a third-party shopping cart that already has a connection to PayPal built into its own APIs. This type of solution usually means that all you have to do is properly configure the cart's settings to plug into the right PayPal account and services.

There are some drawbacks: mainly, you will be at the whim of the transaction flow already established by the shopping cart. If you have unique needs, the shopping cart might accommodate a bit of custom scripting.

But you need to watch how much customization you do; if you end up customizing too much, you may break the cart or may as well have built your own solution anyway.

If the third-party cart works for you, though, it will provide a faster and easier way to integrate a seamless checkout experience into your website, complete with PayPal integration.

Implementing PayPal Integration

When you've decided between HTML- or homegrown API-based payment solutions, you'll need to actually incorporate them into your site. Before beginning, let's examine some of your options for getting this done.

Reviewing the Process

First, here's what you and your development team will need to do for either integration process that you select:

1. For HTML-based solutions, generate the code for the buttons you want to use. For API-based solutions, obtain the code necessary to call the appropriate APIs from your website.

2. Insert the necessary code into the appropriate pages on your website.

3. Test the integration using the PayPal Sandbox testing environment (or your third-party shopping cart site).

NOTE: If you've chosen a third-party shopping cart, you'll need to read the documentation for that product with respect to integrating PayPal.

4. After testing, update your integration configuration as needed.

5. Launch your ecommerce pages.

Getting This Done

Okay, so that doesn't seem so bad. But who has to do all this?

Maybe it will be you. No, seriously.

If you're just adding a few payment buttons on a relatively stable shopping page, and you're halfway familiar with HTML code, there's no reason you can't do this yourself.

> **NOTE:** You can add HTML code directly inside an email or within social media content, as well. This is very simply done in PayPal, and can make purchasing an item very easy.

Doing HTML integration means having the PayPal site create a snippet of HTML code and then inserting that code on your Web page where you want the payment button to appear. If you're comfortable with doing something like this, you can do it yourself.

PayPal INSIDER

Playing in the Sandbox

One of our most popular developer tools is the PayPal Sandbox, a testing environment that duplicates PayPal's live site, without registering real transactions. In essence, the Sandbox lets you use "play money" to test your implementation of PayPal's various HTML buttons and API calls before your site goes live. You can use the Sandbox to test the following:

- Buy Now buttons
- Subscribe buttons
- Donate buttons
- Shopping Cart buttons
- Refunds
- Payment data transfer
- Instant payment notifications
- Simulated transactions

To test in the Sandbox, you must first establish a PayPal Developer Central account. You can then create multiple test accounts for buyers and merchants, so you can simulate different scenarios to be sure that everything functions as expected before launch. Go to developer.paypal.com to access the Sandbox.

To give you an idea of how easy this would be so that you can ascertain your own comfort level, here's what the full code generated by PayPal will essentially look like:

```
<form action="https://www.paypal.com/cgi-bin/webscr" method=
➥"pos t">
<input type="hidden" name="cmd" value="_s-xclick">
<input type="hidden" name="hosted_button_ id" value="value">
<input type" "image" src="https://www.paypal.com/en_US/i/btn/btn_
➥buynowCC_lG.gif" border="0" name="submit" alt="PayPal - The
➥safer, easier way to pay online!">
<img alt="" border="0" src="https://www.paypal.com/en_US/i/scr/
➥pixel.gif" width="1" height="1">
</form>
```

If this code makes sense to you, and you know where to insert it into your Web page's HTML, and how to get that page live on your site, then you're good to go. Remember, PayPal generates the exact code you need to insert; you don't need to write any of this at all.

If you do not understand HTML all that well, or if you simply don't have the time to do it yourself, then you'll need to pass the job off to a Web developer.

This is a task that's pretty easy for an experienced developer and it shouldn't take much time, so it's something for which you can budget lightly. Don't let someone tell you otherwise.

If you already have shopping cart and checkout pages on your site, it's also probably not a big deal for an experienced developer to connect to PayPal using PayPal's API. This is especially true if you find someone who is familiar with PayPal to begin with. APIs aren't hard for pros, but they are not something you want an amateur fooling around with. They will break, or worse, leave a gaping hole in your site's security that can be exploited later.

Finally, if you're already using a third-party shopping cart service that offers PayPal integration, there shouldn't be much, if any, effort on your part. For many businesses, this is probably the easiest way to go. However, if you want to build a custom API-based solution for your site, that will require a lot more development time and effort, so be prepared for that.

Finding the Best Resources

If you do decide to hire a developer to help with your PayPal integration, or you need to add a shopping cart to your site or even build an online store from scratch, PayPal can help. The PayPal Partner Directory can help you find developers to implement solutions. Best of all, these developers are already familiar with PayPal, so they will be familiar with the whole line of PayPal solutions.

NOTE: For more information on social media resources, please see the Appendix, "Social Media Information Resources," in the online chapters.

The Partner Directory can be found at www.paypal.com. Go under the Business tab and click the Partners link. On the Partner Program welcome screen, you'll see the Find a Partner button. Click the button, and PayPal will search for developers and consultants near you (see **Figure 12.3**).

Figure 12.3
Finding developers in the PayPal Partner Directory.

Scroll through the featured partners or filter the list by solutions offered or industries served. Click a partner link to learn more about services offered, and then contact that developer if you want.

Getting Help from PayPal

If you're using in-house staff to implement your PayPal integration, they may need documentation, API calls, and other assistance to get the job done. All of that information—and more—is available on the X.commerce website (www.x.com), seen in **Figure 12.4**.

The X.commerce site, which now houses the PayPal Developer Network, is a developer community organized by PayPal's parent company eBay to foster and enhance ecommerce tool development.

To visit the PayPal Developer Network site, surf to www.x.com/developers/paypal (see **Figure 12.5**). There, you'll want to formally register, although you can get to a lot of the available information as an unregistered guest. Once you've registered, you can use the site to determine the best solution for your business, generate HTML code for payment buttons and the like, download powerful developer tools, access documentation for PayPal's various APIs, view video demos, interact with other developers and PayPal staff in online forums, and utilize many other resources.

Figure 12.4
The X.commerce website.

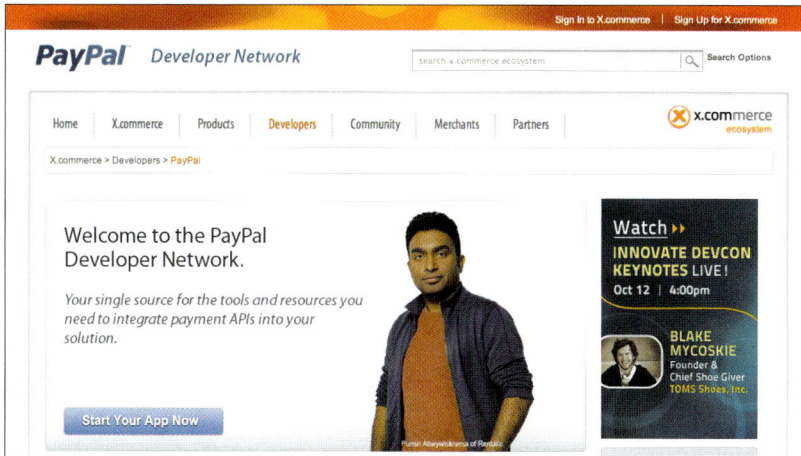

Figure 12.5
*The PayPal
Developer Network
home page.*

The Last Word

There are three ways to integrate PayPal payment processing with your website.

First, there's the simple way: use Web Payments Standard and the HTML code it generates to insert payment buttons on your site. The customer is then sent to PayPal's site to complete the transaction.

Second, use one of the many third-party shopping cart products that already integrates with PayPal (using either Website Payments Standard or Website Payments Pro). This option may require a little configuration, but should not be too arduous.

Last, integrate Website Payments Pro with your new or existing ecommerce system using PayPal's APIs. This approach sends customer information to PayPal for payment processing, but then sends the resulting information back to your website or checkout system in real time. This gives you more control over the checkout process and a seamless user experience, but requires some developer time to be sure everything is coded correctly.

In Chapter 13, "Customizing Payment Options with PayPal," you'll learn how to configure and manage PayPal tools when you are working with a larger ecommerce website.

13

Customizing Payment Options with PayPal

In the previous chapter, you learned the various options you could use to integrate PayPal into your ecommerce site. Now it's time to discover exactly how such integration will work when you have a larger site with many items to sell.

When your company does a lot of business online, you will absolutely need to have a shopping cart system for your customers. To try to duplicate this functionality using plain HTML would be enormously time-consuming. If you don't yet have a shopping cart for your site, PayPal can provide one, at no additional charge and with little effort on your part. Otherwise, you can integrate PayPal's payment processing into your existing shopping cart, including those provided by third-party suppliers.

How Shopping Carts Work

When you have more than one item for sale, your customers will need the option to purchase more than one item at a time, or else they will have to conduct a separate transaction for each item, and you don't want that. (A long time ago, this was actually the norm on the Internet, and thankfully those days are long gone.)

This is the purpose behind a shopping cart: customers can gather up all their purchased items into one "cart," which then feeds into a checkout page where customers provide shipping information and pay for their purchases, just like any brick-and-mortar store.

Checking Out

Shopping carts are really nothing new for online shoppers, but just to make sure we're all on the same page, **Figure 13.1** shows how the process works from the customer's viewpoint, using the PayPal Shopping Cart with Website Payments Standard. The blue-banded pages are hosted on the PayPal site; the gray-banded pages appear on the merchant's site.

Figure 13.1

The three numbered steps are the main parts of the PayPal Shopping Cart checkout process.

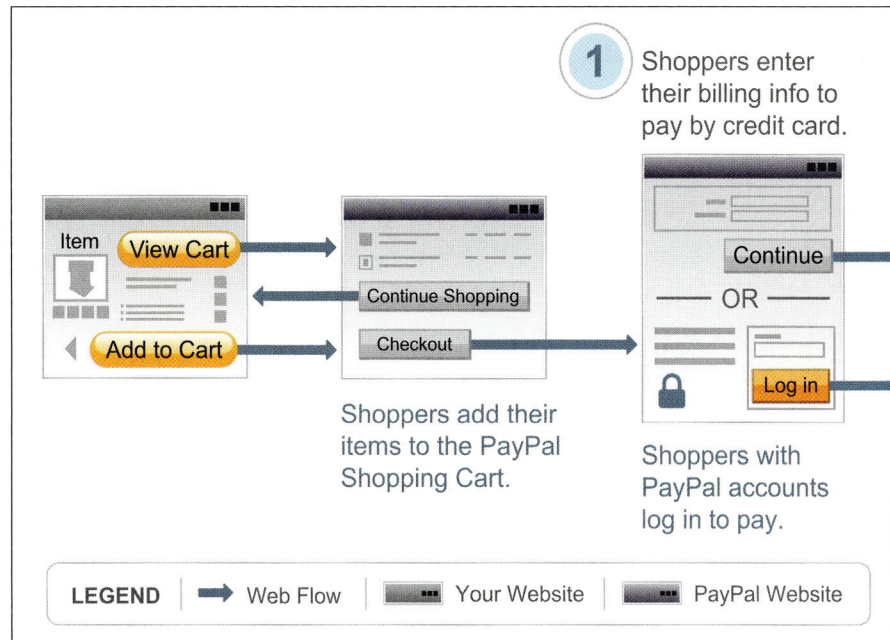

1 Shoppers enter their billing info to pay by credit card.

Item | View Cart | Continue Shopping | Checkout | Add to Cart

Continue — OR — Log in

Shoppers add their items to the PayPal Shopping Cart.

Shoppers with PayPal accounts log in to pay.

LEGEND   ➡ Web Flow   ▮ Your Website   ▮ PayPal Website

The checkout process begins when the customer clicks the Add to Cart button for a particular product. This button is actually hosted on the merchant's website, inserted into the product Web page with HTML, and generated via code supplied by PayPal. Clicking the button adds the item to the shopping cart hosted by PayPal. Now customers can continue shopping—and add more items to the shopping cart—or go directly to the checkout page.

When the checkout button or link is clicked, the customer will be taken to the checkout page hosted by PayPal, although it can be branded by the merchant to give it a look and feel like the rest of the retailer's site. At this point, the customer signs in and either pays with a PayPal account or enters the necessary credit or debit card information. When paying via credit or debit card, the customer also has to enter a shipping address and other relevant information. (These details are already known if the customer pays via a PayPal account.)

The shopper confirms the transaction details and then PayPal processes the payment. If the customer's payment is approved, PayPal generates a

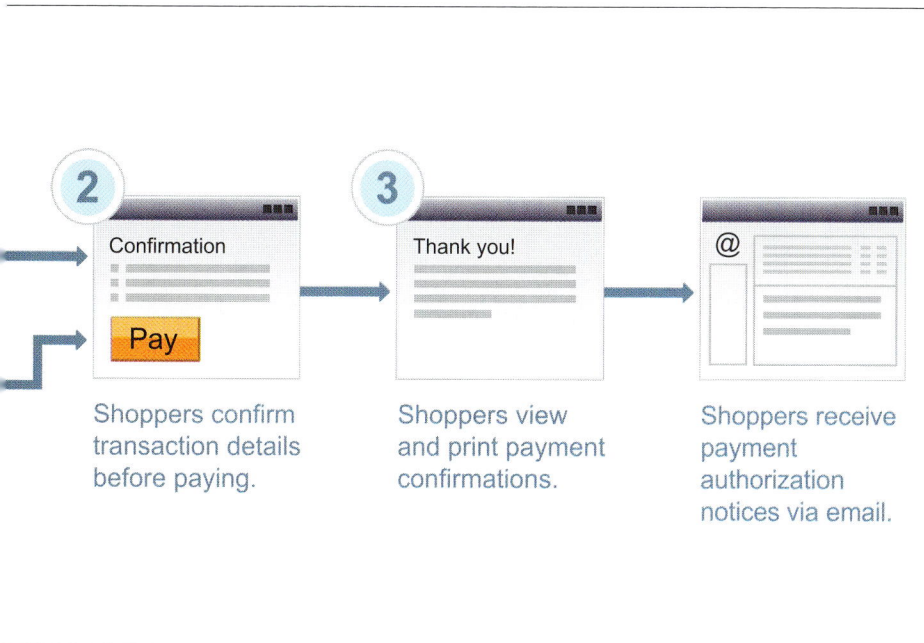

2 Confirmation

Pay

Shoppers confirm transaction details before paying.

3 Thank you!

Shoppers view and print payment confirmations.

@

Shoppers receive payment authorization notices via email.

confirmation screen and transmits information about the purchase to the merchant. The customer is then returned to the merchant's website, and receives (from PayPal) an email confirmation of the purchase.

This is all familiar ground; indeed, we covered it in Chapter 1. But knowing what's really going on here will help you configure PayPal in more efficient ways.

Behind the Scenes

Most shopping cart and checkout systems are built from the following components:

- Payment buttons or links that enable the customer to place individual items into the shopping cart.

- A database that stores information about the products in the customer's shopping cart.

- Web pages that display information about shopping cart contents, and checkout pages that are used when the customer is ready to purchase the items.

- Administrative controls for the shopping cart system.

- Reports that detail shopping cart transactions.

All of these components combine to provide a unified shopping and payment experience for the customer, while allowing you to access and manage your inventory, and providing you with information that triggers the shipment of purchased products.

Of course, all of this is nothing more than an application, just like the ones that run on your computer or smartphone. The only difference is that this application can actually run on one of many locations, thanks to the Internet. It can be on your website's server, or even a third-party's website. PayPal's Shopping Cart runs, naturally, on PayPal's servers.

Because of the speed and ubiquity of most Internet connections, it won't matter where the shopping cart application actually resides (as long as you know it's in a secure spot), because the shopping cart can still be integrated with the rest of your website.

When a customer clicks the Buy Now or Add to Cart button, that information is transmitted to the database part of the shopping cart, which actually keeps track of the items selected. When the customer decides to check out, all items in the database are displayed on a dynamically generated checkout page that pours the information out to the page in real time.

The customer then enters appropriate payment and shipping information, the payment is processed, and the transaction is concluded—all taking place seamlessly in the shopping cart/checkout system.

The product and customer information is stored temporarily in the shopping cart database, but it's not held there for long. The shopping cart system creates the final checkout page on the fly, based on the information stored in the database. Once the transaction is complete, the pertinent information is sent to a more permanent storage tool, usually another database, and additional actions are triggered, such as emails to the warehouse that create pick tickets so the items can be grabbed off the shelves, packed, and shipped, or a message may be sent to your accounting system noting that X items were sold a minute or two ago.

Integrating a Shopping Cart

We touched on shopping cart systems a bit back in Chapter 12, but there are some additional considerations to keep in mind.

If you're using a third-party shopping cart, you need to be sure this application can connect to your existing storefront and inventory systems. If it can't, that's a deal breaker, because if the two systems can't communicate, then you will have to bridge the data gap by entering information manually.

Getting an automated connection requires a fair degree of programming expertise; how much programming is necessary depends on the complexity of the shopping cart and the receiving mercantile servers.

For example, PayPal's Website Payments Standard provides the fully featured PayPal Shopping Cart, all nicely hosted on PayPal. As explained in Chapter 12, all you have to do is insert HTML code for the individual product payments buttons; the checkout process itself resides on the

PayPal site, so you don't have to create new pages for checkout or other activities. The integration process is relatively easy.

If you use another shopping cart solution, however, the integration process can be more complicated. PayPal's Website Payments Pro integrates with most third-party shopping carts, but may require additional programming to implement the necessary calls to various PayPal APIs.

That said, many third-party shopping carts come with PayPal integration built in, which makes it easier for you. Some shopping cart providers have built-in integration with Website Payments Pro; others (those that provide their own merchant credit account solutions) use the gateway approach and tie into PayPal's Payflow Payment Gateway. Either way, integrating PayPal with such a third-party shopping cart offering is often as easy as providing your PayPal credentials to the shopping cart service and checking a few options on a sign-up form.

Do You Need a Shopping Cart Partner?

Let's say you're too big for an HTML-based solution like PayPal's Website Payments Standard. This is one of those problems that's nice to have, though you won't think so at the time. When it comes to implementing a shopping cart on your site, you have three basic options.

- **Build your own shopping cart from scratch.** This is expensive and time consuming, and that's an understatement. The advantage is that you'll get a totally customized solution that exactly matches the look and feel of the rest of your website. The disadvantage is that your bank account might be somewhat depleted when you're done, so be ready to sell lots of things.

  Your own shopping cart also means that you can forego any monthly or usage fees that you would have to pay to a third-party checkout vendor. You'll still have to pay a payment-processing vendor, such as PayPal, naturally.

- **Use the PayPal Shopping Cart.** This is the easiest solution to implement: all you have to do is generate and insert Add to Shopping Cart button codes for each SKU on your site; PayPal handles everything else. There's no integration programming necessary, beyond placing the HTML code for your buttons on the site. It's also free. The PayPal Shopping Cart has no setup fees and no ongoing monthly fees. (You do have to pay PayPal's normal payment processing fees, of course.)

- **Use a third-party shopping cart service.** These services offer ready-to-run shopping cart/checkout systems that can be customized in look and feel to match the rest of your site, especially if your site is built upon one of the popular Content Management Systems (CMS), such as Drupal, Joomla!, or WordPress. This is a middle-of-the-road approach: the integration is less complex than if you were to build a checkout system from the ground up, but you're still going to need a fair bit of programming to get the functionality integrated into your site.

- **There are usually ongoing fees.** You'll pay a set monthly fee for the use of the shopping cart; per-transaction fees or fees based on your transaction volume; as well as the usual payment processing fees.

How do you implement each of these solutions? It depends on which choice you make.

Building It Yourself

If you want to build it yourself, you'll need to contract with a Web development firm—ideally, the same folks building the rest of your site, since they'll know where all the hooks are. Make sure that you're dealing with a firm that has experience building ecommerce sites and systems.

Finding a Shopping Cart Partner

If you do decide to work with a third-party shopping cart, the PayPal Partner Directory can help you find the right vendor.

The Partner Directory can be found at www.paypal.com; under the Business tab, click the Partners link. On the Partner Program welcome screen, you'll see the Find a Partner button. Click the button, and PayPal will search for developers and consultants near you. After you see the results, select the Shopping Cart option in the Solution Types pane on the left side of the screen. This will display a shopping-cart specific vendor (see **Figure 13.2**).

PayPal INSIDER

Content Management Systems

Most small- to medium-sized online businesses do fine with a static website and shopping cart system. But if you have hundreds or thousands of SKUs, you may be better off with a more sophisticated content management system and product database. This type of system doesn't rely on static product Web pages; instead, all product information is stored in a large database, and product pages are generated dynamically when a customer browses to or searches for a particular SKU. You enter information about each product into the database, and that information is then fed into a template used for each product page.

From the customer's viewpoint, a CMS-based site looks identical to a site based on static product pages. The only visible difference is the page URL, which is short and static on a normal site, but is dynamically generated on a CMS site and can be long.

From your perspective, a CMS-based site can be difficult to implement, at least initially. It requires quite a bit of initial coding, as well as the creation of a product database. But many sites on the Web are moving to a CMS approach with the popularity of PHP:Hypertext Preprocessor-based open source systems such as Drupal, Joomla!, and WordPress, which makes maintaining pages at your site easier. Our own X.commerce site, for instance, is built on Drupal.

For ecommerce specifically, ongoing maintenance is easier since you can add new products (and new product pages) simply by adding more information to the database. Changing the price value in the database means the new price is automatically reflected in all dynamically generated product pages.

Starting with a CMS or migrating to a CMS is a great idea if your inventory greatly increases in size. If you expect this to happen, then implementing a CMS early in your ecommerce process will be a great way to plan ahead.

In terms of integrating with a shopping cart, CMS-based systems have gotten highly sophisticated and a lot simpler to use as time has gone by, and there are a lot of ready-to-use ecommerce systems that plug right into existing CMS-built sites with little to no configuration needed, which makes them a definite solution to examine.

Figure 13.2
Finding shopping cart partners in the PayPal Partner Directory.

Scroll through the featured partners and click a partner link to learn more about services offered, and then contact that developer if you want.

Selecting the PayPal Shopping Cart

The PayPal Shopping Cart is available with Website Payments Standard. When you sign up for your PayPal account, this is the solution you want to choose. It lets your customers purchase multiple items on your site, as opposed to the Buy Now button, which is a single-item-only tool.

After you've signed up to PayPal, integrating the Pay Pal Shopping Cart into your site is a simple matter of generating HTML code for an Add to Cart button for each SKU on your site, and then inserting that code into each product page. (**Figure 13.3** shows typical results.) You'll also want to generate code for and insert View Cart buttons (also shown in Figure 13.3), so that your customers can check out and pay when they're ready.

Figure 13.3
PayPal's Add to Cart and View Cart buttons on a sample page.

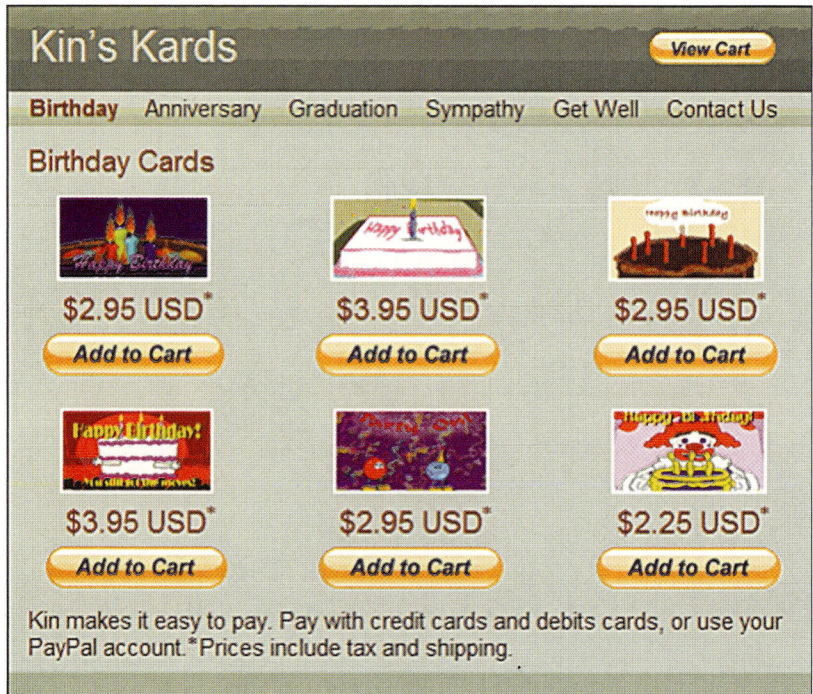

Once all the buttons are generated and inserted and you take your new product pages live, your shopping cart is also live. Since all the processing occurs on PayPal's site, your setup work is now done; any customer who makes a purchase will use the PayPal Shopping Cart.

NOTE: Learn more about creating payment buttons in Chapter 12, "Integrating PayPal with Websites."

Configuring the PayPal Shopping Cart

Implementing the PayPal Shopping Cart isn't hard, but there are quite a few payment options you need to configure, such as tax rate, shipping charges, and so on. While you can specify some of these settings on an

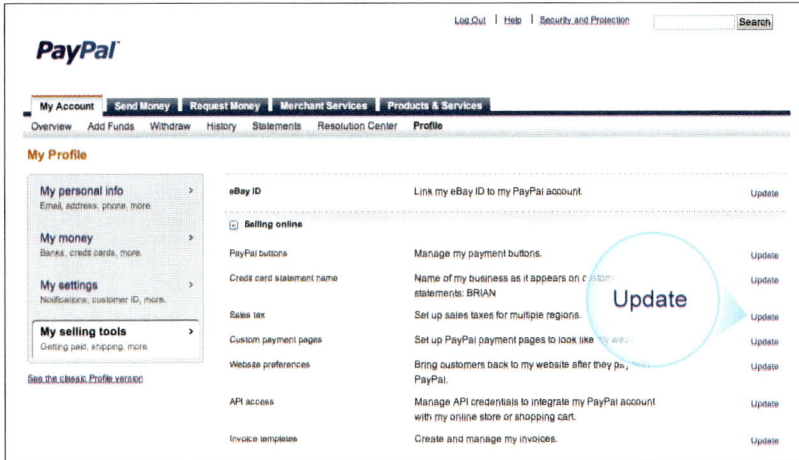

Figure 13.4
The Selling Online section of your PayPal account profile.

item- or SKU-specific basis when you create the product's Add to Cart button, most settings (like sales tax) should be applied universally to your entire shopping cart.

You configure these universal payment settings under the Selling Online section of your profile, shown in **Figure 13.4**. To open these controls, log in to your PayPal account, click the My Account tab, and then click the Profile link. On the My Profile page that appears, select the My Selling Tools option in the left-hand sidebar.

Figuring Taxes

As an online business, you may or may not be required to charge sales tax on the items you sell; it depends largely on what kind of traditional retail presence you have and where you are shipping. Some states require sales tax, some don't. Before you make the decision, consult a tax attorney, because you will want to be very sure before you run afoul of your state revenue office.

1. If you have to charge taxes, click the Update link next to the Sales Tax option in the Selling Online section of My Profile. The Sales Tax page will be displayed, as shown in **Figure 13.5**.

Figure 13.5
The Sales Tax page.

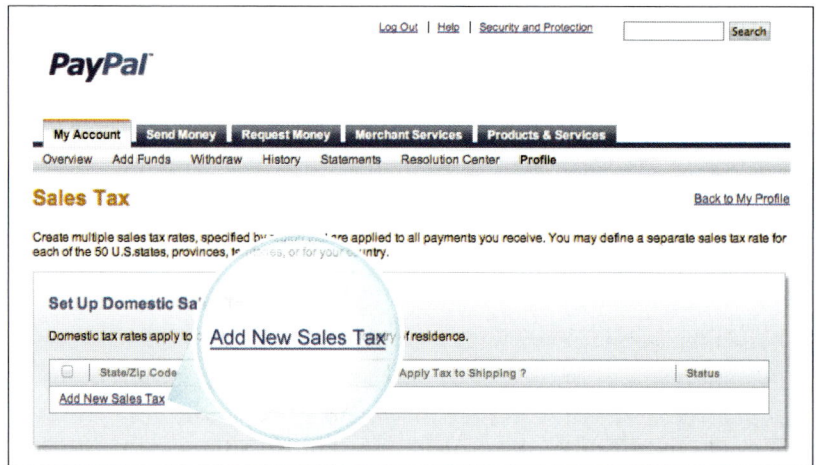

2. In the Set Up Domestic Sales Tax Rates section, click the Add New Sales Tax link. The Domestic Sales Tax page will appear (see **Figure 13.6**).

Figure 13.6
The Domestic Sales Tax page.

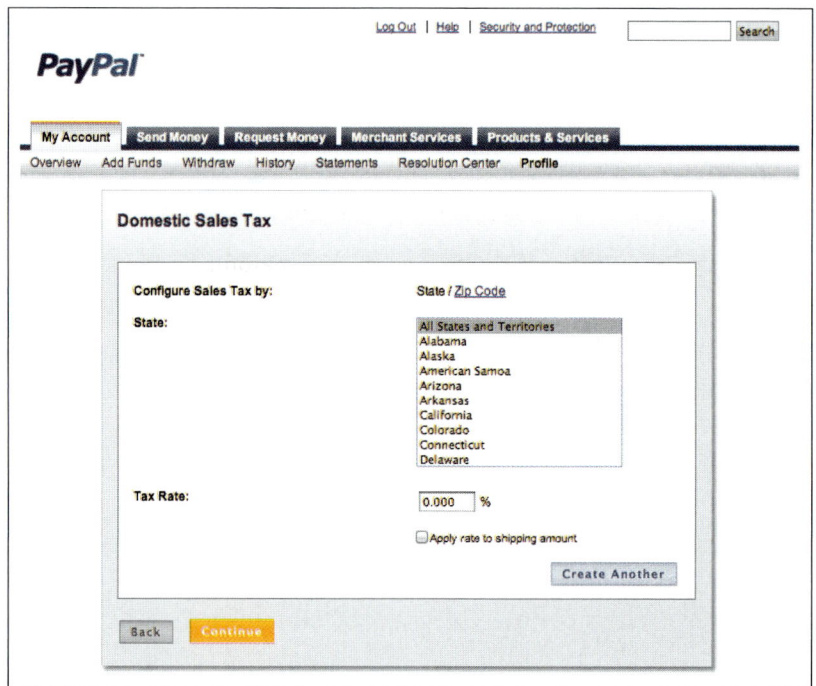

3. Select a state and enter the applicable tax rate for that state in the Tax Rate field.

4. If you need to apply sales tax for a specific city or county, click the Zip Code link and enter the ZIP code.

By default, the sales tax is applied only to the product price; if tax must be applied to the entire purchase price, including shipping, check the Apply Rate to Shipping Amount box.

In most instances, you charge sales tax only for those states in which you have a physical presence. If you have a physical presence in multiple states, you'll have to specify tax rates for each state in which you do business. Click the Create Another button to add another state to your list. When you're done specifying tax rates, click the Continue button.

TIP: If sales tax is different for a specific item, you can set a product-specific tax rate when you're creating that item's Add to Cart button. Just enter the applicable tax rate into the Tax Rate box when you create the button.

Determining Shipping and Handling Fees

You can also set universal shipping and handling fees in My Profile.

1. In the Shipping My Items section on your My Profile page, click the Update link next to the Shipping Calculations option; this displays the Shipping Calculations page, shown in **Figure 13.7**.

Figure 13.7
The Shipping Calculations tool.

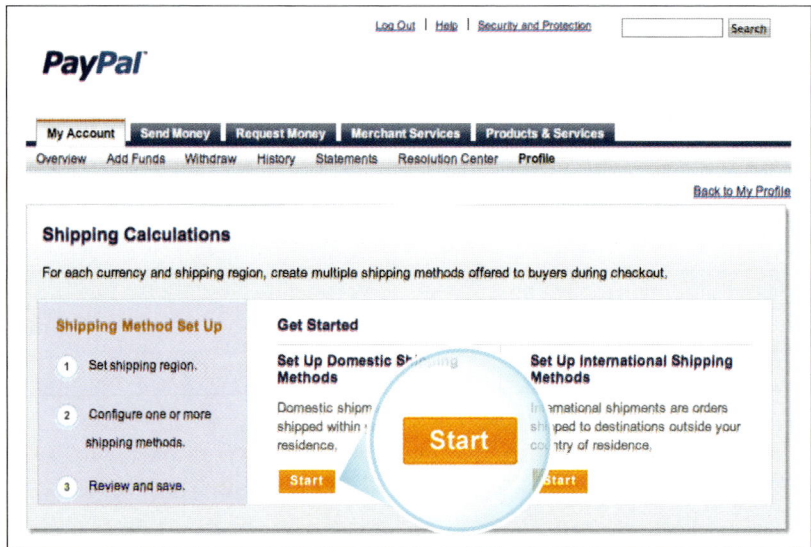

2. Click the Start button in the Set Up Domestic Shipping Methods section. The Shipping Region page will appear (see **Figure 13.8**).

Figure 13.8
Set shipping regions on the Shipping Region page.

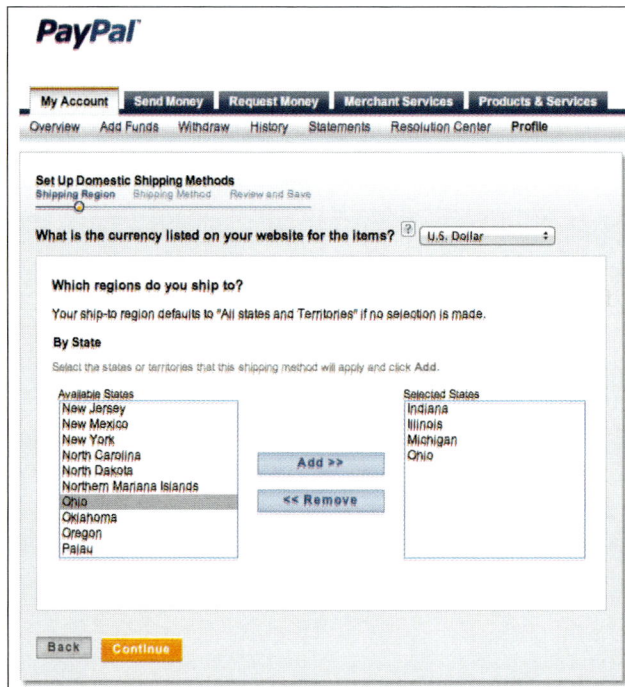

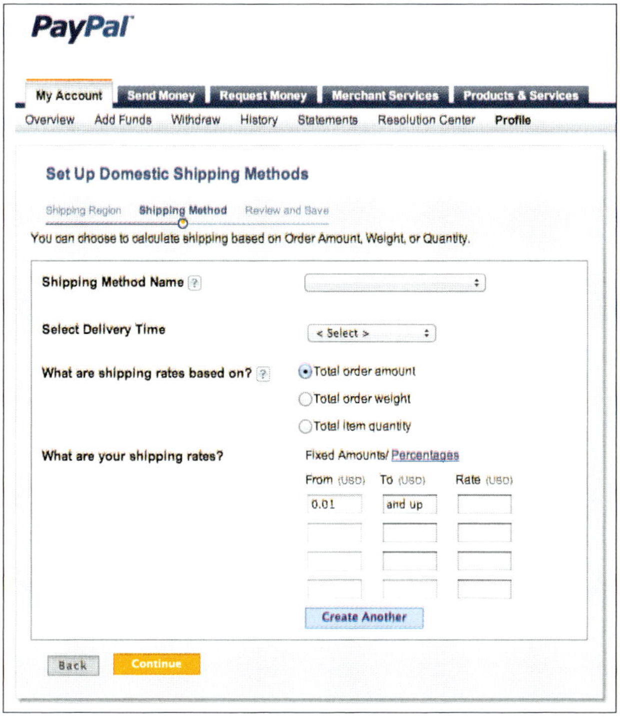

Figure 13.9
The Shipping Method page.

3. Click the states you ship to and click the Add button.

4. When the states you want are in the Selected States field, click Continue. The Shipping Method page will appear (see **Figure 13.9**).

5. Select a shipping method, set your standard delivery time, specify how your rates are based (on total order amount, weight, or quantity), and then specify your shipping rates, either by dollar amount or percentage.

6. To create multiple shipping fee schedules for multiple shipping methods, click the Create Another button.

7. Click Continue. The Review and Save page will appear.

8. If what you see is correct, click the Save Shipping Methods button.

Receiving Notice of Payment

Perhaps the best message you can find in your inbox is a note saying that someone's actually bought one of your products, and you need to ship a product right away.

When you use the PayPal Shopping Cart, you will be notified by email of any transaction PayPal handles for you. If you've connected PayPal to another shopping cart system, PayPal can notify the shopping cart directly and send you a notification.

Notification events include:

- Instant payments, including direct credit card payments. These payments are conducted and transmitted nearly instantaneously.

- E-check payments, which enable users to pay directly from their checking account with their account information and their status.

- Recurring payments and subscription events.

- Chargebacks, disputes, reversals, and refunds.

If you're using a more sophisticated ecommerce system, you may be able to take advantage of PayPal's Instant Payment Notification (IPN), which automatically notifies your ecommerce system of all PayPal events.

NOTE: IPN messages duplicate messages sent via email, so you're well covered on transaction information.

IPN messages are detected and processed via a listener script or program that is integrated into your ecommerce system. (Your developer will need to write the listener scripts.) When the script receives an IPN message, it then passes that message to the appropriate process to respond to the message.

For example, an IPN message about a customer purchase can trigger order-fulfillment processes, update your customer list, and update your accounting records, all automatically. You can configure the IPN messages received by clicking the Instant Payment Notification Preferences link on your profile.

Configuring Other Options

There are several other options you can configure from the My Selling Tools area of your PayPal profile. These include the following:

- **Selling Online.** This section includes a variety of links to help you manage your online selling activities. Besides setting up your sales tax settings, you can manage your PayPal payment buttons; change the company name that appears on your customers' credit card statements; configure PayPal payment pages to look more like your own site; determine which Web pages customers are directed to after they pay with PayPal; manage API credentials for integrating PayPal with your own online store or shopping cart; and create and manage your invoice templates.

- **Getting Paid and Managing My Risk.** This section includes a variety of links to help you manage customer payments. From here, you can manage subscriptions and other automatic payments: integrate PayPal's instant payment notifications with your site; manage PayPal's risk and fraud controls to automatically accept or decline certain types of payments; block payments based on specified criteria; and create a personalized message to use when faced with customer disputes.

- **Shipping My Items.** This section helps you configure PayPal's shipping functionality. From here, you can edit your shipping preferences, including carriers and labels, as well as set up shipping methods and pricing for each of your customers.

You'll also find links to additional selling tools, including encrypted payment settings, PayPal button language encoding, PayPal shops, and your seller reputation number.

NOTE: Your seller reputation number reflects the number of unique verified PayPal members who have paid you. The higher that number, typically the more trustworthy you are.

The three other entries on the left panel of your profile pertain to any PayPal member—they are not specific to a business that is selling through PayPal. These are:

- **My Business Info.** Where you edit your contact information such as an email address, phone number, and so on.

- **My Money.** Where you set your payment and banking information, including credit card and bank account numbers.

- **My Settings.** Where you will find your basic account settings such as notifications, customer ID, and so on.

TIP: Magento is an ecommerce solution offering flexibility and control over the look, content, and functionality of an online store (www.magentocommerce.com/). It's fast to install, has a full suite of features, and is free to download. Merchants and developers who integrate Magento's services will have automatic access to PayPal's payment engine. You can create a Magento-hosted store, where all backend services and functionality are managed by Magento, or deploy a storefront using Magento's rich set of tools and services.

The Last Word

For most online merchants, customers pay via an online shopping cart and checkout system. You can decide how much effort to put into your ecommerce site, and how much return you will get.

Ultimately, you should focus your efforts on making the ecommerce process as painless as possible. After establishing a good dialogue with your customers via social media, you don't want to hurt the relationship with a poorly designed checkout system.

In Chapter 14, "Securing Your Transactions," we'll raise the issue your customers are really worried about when it comes to online shopping: security.

14

Securing Your Transactions

If you're in business, then sadly you know a thing or two about fraud. Criminal activity, whether shoplifting or counterfeit money, has been a problem since the very first store opened. The problem hasn't gone away with the advent of online commerce. In fact, many would argue that the problem has worsened due to the increased anonymity inherent with the Internet.

Whatever your organization's goals, profit or non-profit, it's critical to protect yourself as much as possible from criminal and fraudulent activity. It's even more important while working with social media. Luckily, PayPal offers a variety of anti-fraud programs and services that help to minimize the effects of online criminals.

Understanding Fraud

It's a common misconception that a lot of online fraud out there is simply a "victimless" crime. Sure, a consumer may get stuck with a huge credit card bill of bad transactions, but they usually get fixed and the consumer isn't usually liable, depending on the card used and the bank's liability clause, people will argue.

But there are consequences, which can ripple back to the merchants either indirectly through credit card banks raising fees or higher insurance premiums, or directly through penalties and fees—sometimes as much as $30 per fraudulent transaction.

There is no such thing as a victimless crime. One way or the other, when something is stolen, somebody pays.

The Scope of Online Fraud

According to the Internet Crime Complaint Center (IC3), a joint FBI/Department of Justice Internet watchdog organization, 2010 had the second highest number of complaints since the IC3's inception in 2001, although that's fallen from the all-time high in 2009. So while people are getting wiser about online fraud, it's also clear that the scammers are still clever, too.

The IC3's 2010 annual report (www.ic3.gov/media/annualreport/2010_IC3Report.pdf) lays it all out: non-delivery of payment or merchandise was the number one type of Internet crime in 2010 (as evidenced by the fact that it comprised 21.5 percent of all complaints). Identity theft came in at number two with 16.6 percent, auction fraud was third at 10.1 percent, and credit card fraud was fourth at 9.3 percent.

Crime has indeed changed: once, online auction fraud was the top complaint at the IC3. But now, with social media providing so many avenues for scammers to contact people, criminals can be very creative in how they find new ways to part you or others from your money or goods.

Types of Online Fraud

So just how creative are these criminal types? Very much so, sadly. Here are a just a few of the possible situations that an online merchant might encounter:

- **No item received.** A scammer purchases an item from you, the merchant. You ship it to the customer. The customer then claims that he never received the item and asks for a refund. If you refund the money, you're docked the cost of the item plus the item itself—and the scammer has a brand-new item obtained at no cost. If you send the customer a replacement item, he has two no-cost items, which he can sell or use at his convenience.

- **Item is not as described.** This is a similar scam to the "no item received" scam. The perpetrator purchases an item from you. You ship the item, and then the customer claims that the item isn't what was described. It's used instead of new, the wrong size, doesn't have the features promised, or is otherwise not what he ordered. To satisfy the customer, you issue a full or partial refund, which docks you the cost of the original item plus the cost of the refund. The scammer, of course, has a nice new product at no cost or at a reduced price.

- **Item was damaged in shipment.** This is a variation of the "not as described" scam. You ship to the scammer the item purchased, and then the customer claims that the item was damaged in transit. Rather than dealing with the shipping service, you issue a full or partial refund. (Or maybe you issue a refund in advance, anticipating settlement from the shipping service.) The scammer gets an undamaged item at a substantial discount.

- **Check or money order fraud.** Also known as an overpayment scam, the fraud works something like this: a merchant sells an item, and the buyer pays for the item with a cashier's check or money order. But there's a problem; the buyer tells the merchant that he's mistakenly sent too large a check. Could the merchant send the excess amount back with the item? Because it's a cashier's check or money order, banks will normally release the funds in just a day or so, giving the merchant the impression that the funds have cleared. In reality, the check or money order is fake, but it can take up to weeks for your bank to learn this, and you've already sent the "extra" funds back to the buyer days before, along with the merchandise he bought. Since PayPal doesn't process checks or money orders, their services don't apply in this case, but it's a good idea for you to remain alert about such fraud.

- **The buyer pays with a stolen credit card or a hijacked bank account.** The previous scams are all pretty much single events, because they're only going to work with you once. A much more damaging form of fraud comes from actual identity theft, where a criminal steals a customer's credit card or debit card, or somehow hijacks the customer's bank account. The criminal then uses the stolen data or information to make one or more purchases, typically large ones, from you (and other merchants). It looks like a standard transaction from your end, and you ship the merchandise—typically to a realistic address, where someone acts as a freight forwarder, receiving illegally obtained merchandise and then shipping it to locales where the criminals can then use or dispose of the merchandise as they see fit. When the original consumer—the one whose identity was stolen—notices the fraudulent account activity and makes a formal complaint, the consumer's credit card company or bank initiates a chargeback against you, the merchant, to recover the consumer's funds. This activity typically results in you being docked the cost of the fraudulently obtained merchandise and having the sales price for said items deducted from your merchant credit account.

> ⚠ **CAUTION:** Who gets the bill? You do! Most credit processing agreements hold online merchants liable for any losses incurred from fraudulent credit card payments.

- **Corporate identity theft.** Identity theft isn't just for individuals. Many businesses find that criminals somehow obtain usernames, passwords, and other information that lets them either hack into others' accounts or systems or make purchases while pretending to be someone authorized by your business. In the best-case scenario (and it's not so good), the thieves order various items and you pay for them. In the worst-case scenario, the criminals hack into your internal systems and wreak havoc, up to and including stealing your customers' personal data and shutting down your systems and servers.

Identity Theft 101

As you can see, the most damaging forms of online fraud involve some form of ID theft—either of your ID or your customers' IDs. How, exactly, do criminals obtain this information?

Identity theft is not exclusively an online activity. You can be as careful online as you want, only to learn that someone pulled your credit card statements from the trash bins behind your shop.

In fact, getting IDs is often a rather mundane activity, as thieves may attempt the following:

- Stealing a person's wallet or purse.

- Stealing a company's or individual's mail, in particular bank and credit card statements. Or stealing those pre-approved credit card offers that arrive in the post, unsolicited.

- Completing a change of address form with the U.S. Postal Service to divert a person's mail to another location.

- Rummaging through a business's or an individual's trash for key financial records.

- Stealing an individual's or a company's credit report by posing as a landlord or employer.

- Conning a company's human resources department into providing a person's personnel records.

- Buying personal or company information from inside sources, typically store or company employees.

Of course, there's going to be some online theft, so don't let your guard down. Online criminals can also do the following:

- Use malware on your computers, such as "packet sniffer" software, to obtain passwords and numbers while you are online.

- Purchase or otherwise obtain illegally gathered information from an underground website or Internet Relay Chat (IRC) channel, usually run by large criminal syndicates.

- Use social engineering and phishing techniques to con people into providing confidential information via phone, email, instant messaging, and, yes, social networking sites. Many people can publish information on social media sites, such as their full birth date, that can help fraudsters.

NOTE: "Phishing" is an active attempt to fool unsuspecting victims into providing key financial information. Usually, this is done by impersonating a trusted entity—even PayPal. The one thing you should always know: no official representative of any site will ever ask for your password and login information.

In short, there are a lot of different ways that identity-based information can be stolen. And once stolen, that information can be used to commit fraud against your business.

Reducing Online Fraud

Most merchants can't afford the financial losses caused by fraudulent transactions. And, honestly, even if you could, why would you want to? You need to take aggressive steps to minimize fraud. Here are some ways you can help your business:

- **Ship only to confirmed addresses.** Criminals who hijack consumers' accounts typically ship the illicit merchandise to some other address— not to the original consumer. To make the address look legit, they will use freight forwarders—sometimes duped staffers who will forward those goods on to addresses with less savory track records. Even so, be on the lookout for address inconsistencies, especially orders that have you sending the merchandise to an address other than the one that originally was recorded for a customer. Especially suspicious are orders that have a billing address in one country and a shipping address in another.

- **Track all packages.** This is a great way to help protect against scammers who claim not to have received a package. Get shipping or delivery confirmation, and you have a good defense against this type of scam.

- **Insure all packages.** Help protect yourself against claims of shipping damage by purchasing insurance for all the items you ship. This way you're protected if an item actually does get damaged in shipment—or if a recipient claims that the package arrived damaged.

- **Beware of unusual customer requests.** Beware of any suspicious requests on an order, such as customers willing to pay any price for rush delivery, split payments made from different PayPal accounts or credit cards, payments sent piecemeal from the same PayPal account, orders that are not paid for in a single, full payment, or payments that are too big and the buyer asks you to send something back. You should also be suspicious of orders—especially from new customers—that are substantially larger than your typical order, or are for multiple items of the same style, color, or size. All of these are red flags that something foul may be afoot.

- **Know your buyers.** You also need to know to whom you're selling. Make sure that new customers have a verified PayPal account and a confirmed address before you ship.

What do you do if you receive a suspicious order online? A good first step is to call the customer to confirm. You can also take advantage of PayPal's various anti-fraud services, which we'll discuss next.

Using PayPal's Anti-Fraud Services

PayPal offers a variety of services and technologies designed to identify and help prevent fraudulent transactions, including a team of more than 2,000 specialists working 24/7 on your behalf, as well as highly effective anti-fraud risk models and detection techniques that help stop fraud in its tracks.

Fighting Fraud Online with PayPal

What measures does PayPal take to help reduce fraud? There are many, including the following:

- Address confirmation to protect against packages being shipped to places other than the legitimate customer's residence or place of business.

> **NOTE:** PayPal verifies the customer's credit card billing address; shipping to an address other than this confirmed address is not advised.

- Strong data encryption, to keep hackers from stealing transmitted data—and to keep merchant transactions and financial information private.

- Integrated shipping and package tracking capabilities, so you know that your packages get where they're supposed to go.

- Transaction screening to alert merchants of suspicious account activity, using sophisticated fraud models to identify potentially fraudulent transactions before they're completed.

- Industry-standard Address Verification Service (AVS) and Credit Card Verification Value (CVV2) checks as additional layers of protection against identity theft.

- Dispute-resolution assistance for all sellers, through the PayPal Resolution Center. The Resolution Center offers fair and speedy resolution for any dispute that should occur between buyers and sellers. This helps to ward off unwarranted refunds and chargebacks—often before they reach the need for a chargeback.

- A full-time chargeback-fighting team, focused on denying fraudulent chargebacks from unscrupulous buyers.

PayPal's Anti-Fraud Team

In addition to various anti-fraud tools and technologies, PayPal offers highly trained security teams that help keep your sensitive data private and your transactions more secure. These professionals work behind the scenes, monitoring activity and possible fraud indicators to ensure a safer transaction network.

PayPal's fraud experts also work closely with the FBI and other law enforcement agencies to identify and combat fraud wherever it occurs. PayPal's team is charged with making every PayPal transaction as secure and as seamless as possible—for all parties.

Should PayPal's fraud experts identify suspicious activity regarding one of your transactions, the transaction is placed on hold for 24 hours while the risk team determines its validity. PayPal will also alert you by email or have a representative call you, so you can then take whatever action is appropriate.

Using Fraud Management Filters

If you use one of PayPal's payment processing products, you're protected by multiple Fraud Management filters. These filters are tools to identify payment characteristics that may indicate fraudulent activity.

If a transaction is flagged by one of these filters, you then have the option of denying incoming payments that are likely to result in fraudulent transactions, or of accepting payments that are not typically a problem. If you are using the Website Payments Pro feature, you can even decide to further investigate flagged transactions, by comparing prior orders, for example, or by contacting the customer for more information.

This is good, because *time* is the one thing that scammers don't have on their side. The slower and more patient you are with an odd transaction, the more likely that someone who is up to some fraudulent behavior will get caught.

Benefiting from Fraud Management Filters

PayPal provides free filters for all business accounts. These basic filters screen against the country of origin, the value of transactions, and other key indicators that will protect you from really obvious fraudulent activity.

When you subscribe to Website Payments Pro, you will have access to more advanced filters (available at an additional charge). These filters screen against credit card and address information, lists of high-risk indicators, and additional fraudulent transaction characteristics, such as nations known to have increased criminal activity.

How Fraud Management Filters Work

Figure 14.1 shows how Fraud Management filters typically work. In essence, there are three steps involved:

1. You, the merchant, configure your specific Fraud Management filters to either flag or hold for review suspicious transactions, or to deny riskier payments outright.

2. Based on the settings you specify, your filters will review all incoming payments.

3. Your filters automatically flag, hold for review, or deny payments, as specified.

As an example, consider the Country Monitor filter. Let's say you specify that no orders should come from countries known to have a high rate of fraudulent activity; any orders coming from such a nation are flagged for

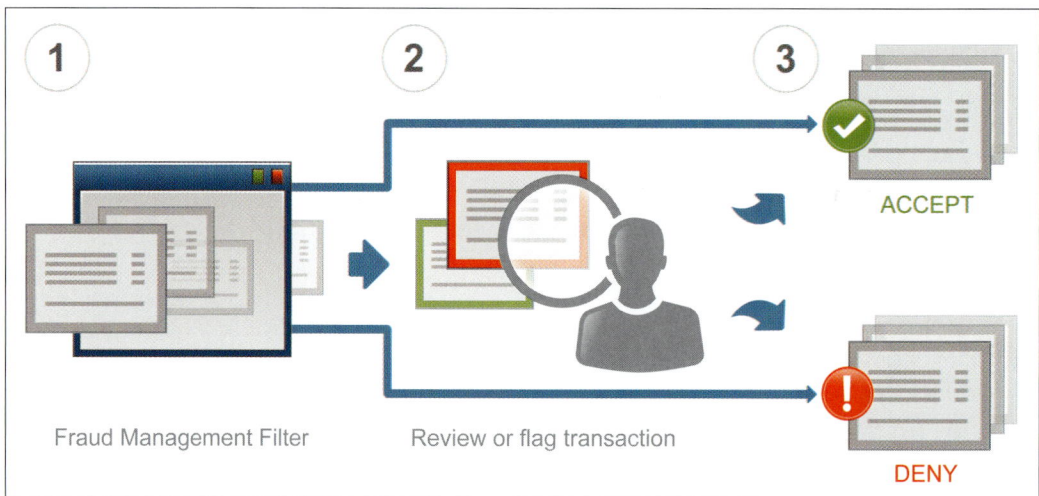

Figure 14.1 *The three steps involved with a Fraud Management filter.*

review. When a criminal using a stolen ID tries to ship an order to one of those countries, the order is flagged, and the merchant will get an email notifying him of the problem. The merchant can take the step of calling the customer to confirm where the item should be shipped. When the legitimate individual answers the phone, the merchant and the customer will discover the attempted criminal activity.

You can then deny the fraudulent transaction, and the victim of identity theft takes action to stop further purchases on the stolen credit card.

Usually, most payments are accepted by the filters because they don't show the characteristics you designated and thus do not indicate fraud. Those payments that are potentially fraudulent, however, are stopped and dealt with in the method you specify.

Evaluating Fraud Management Filters

What Fraud Management filters are offered? It depends on which PayPal product you use.

NOTE: If you use a third-party shopping cart provider, consult with your vendor to see which PayPal Fraud Management filters are supported.

All PayPal business users have access to the following three basic filters at no additional cost:

- **Country Monitor filter.** Identifies transactions based on the country of origin.

- **Maximum Transaction Amount filter.** Identifies transactions that exceed a value specified by the merchant.

- **Unconfirmed Address filter.** Screens for payments above a specified amount when the shipping address entered by the customer has not yet been confirmed by PayPal.

Website Payments Pro subscribers have access to the following advanced filters, at an additional cost per month:

- **Address Verification Partial Match filter.** Screens for transactions where the billing address entered by the customer doesn't completely match the information maintained by the card issuer.

- **Address Verification Service No Match filter.** Screens for transactions where the billing address entered by the customer doesn't match the information provided by the card issuer.

- **Address Verification Service Unavailable or Not Supported filter.** Filters for instances where the Address Verification Service (AVS) is unable to verify the billing address.

- **Bank Identification Number filter.** Scans for payments from credit cards with Bank Identification Numbers (BINs) that have historically been associated with a high rate of fraudulent transactions. BINs, which identify the bank issuing the card, are checked against a "Risk List" maintained by PayPal.

- **Billing/Shipping Address Mismatch filter.** Looks for payments with different billing and shipping addresses.

- **Card Security Code Mismatch filter.** Identifies transactions with differences in the credit card security code.

- **Email Address Domain filter.** Screens for email addresses with historically high rates of fraud, using a "Risk List" of email domains maintained by PayPal.

- **IP Address Range filter.** Targets payments from Internet Protocol (IP) addresses that have historically high instances of fraud, using a "Risk List" maintained by PayPal.

- **IP Address Velocity filter.** Screens for multiple payments made in a short amount of time from the same IP address.

- **Large Order Number filter.** Locates transactions based on the number of items purchased, seeking larger-than-normal quantities.

- **PayPal Fraud Model filter.** Screens for payments that would have been declined by PayPal's fraud model.

- **Suspected Freight Forwarder filter.** Searches for payments where the shipping address is a known freight forwarder, using a "Risk List" of U.S. shipping addresses maintained by PayPal.

- **Total Purchase Price Minimum filter.** Identifies transactions that are less than a specified amount.

- **Zip Code filter.** Sorts for billing addresses that have historically high rates of fraud using a "Risk List" of U.S. shipping addresses maintained by PayPal.

NOTE: Available filters are determined by an agreement between you and PayPal; not all merchants are eligible to see all filters.

Understanding Filter Settings

You can configure each individual Fraud Management filter to one of four action settings: automatically accept or deny a transaction, or review or flag a transaction. Table 14.1 details each of these settings.

Table 14.1 Fraud Management Filter Settings

Action Setting	Description
Accept	Accepts the payment. This setting is used only by the Total Purchase Price Minimum filter, and it instructs PayPal to accept transactions that fall below a minimum transaction amount.
Deny	Denies the payment. Use this setting only if you're positive you want the associated filter to automatically disqualify the payment. For example, you might use this setting to deny payments from buyers in countries with which it's too risky or difficult to conduct business.
Review	Makes the payment pending your review. Use this setting when you want to evaluate the transaction and then make a case-by-case decision on whether to accept or deny the payment.
Flag	Accepts the payment but flags it for later evaluation. This is a good setting to use when first testing the effect of a filter, or when you're not sure you want to review the payment but want an easy way to locate the flagged payment, should you decide to examine it.

Activating Fraud Management Filters

To use the filters listed in the previous section, you need to set them up. If you have a basic business account, there will only be three filters to configure.

To set up filters in a basic account, follow these steps:

1. In the Profile section of the My Account page, click the My Selling Tools link in the left sidebar. The Selling Tools options will appear.

2. In the Getting Paid and Managing My Risk section, click the Update link next to the Block Payments option. The Payment Receiving Preferences page will appear, as seen in Figure 14.2.

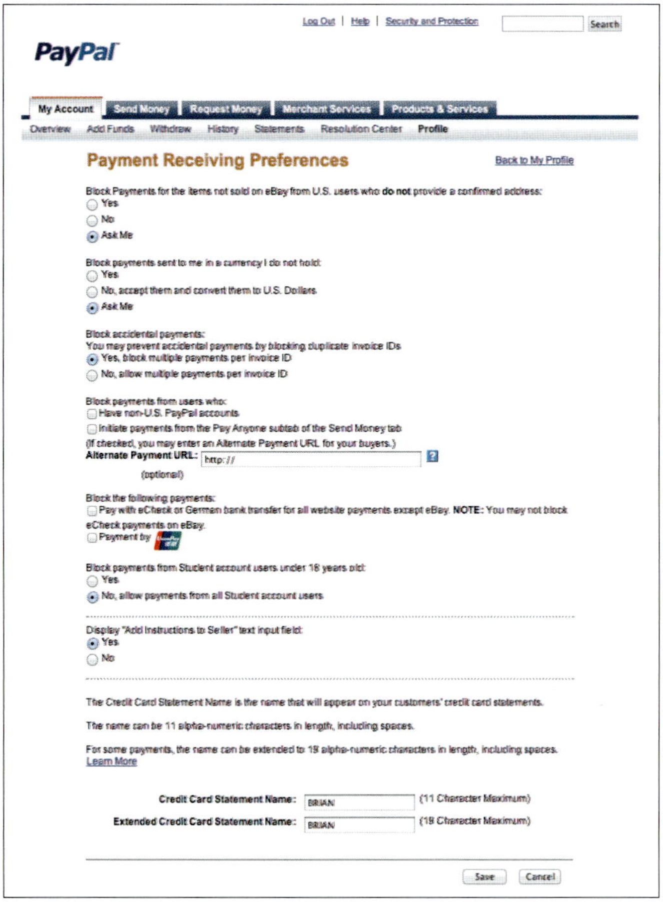

Figure 14.2
Activating Fraud Management filters in a basic account.

3. Select Yes for the payment receipt options that you want to activate.

4. Click Save. Your payment filter options will be configured.

Since a more advanced business account will have more Fraud Management filters, you will need to follow these steps:

1. In the Profile section of the My Account page, click the My Selling Tools link in the left sidebar. The selling tools options will appear.

2. In the Getting Paid and Managing My Risk section, click the Update link next to the Managing Risk and Fraud option. The Edit My Filter Settings page will appear, similar to the one shown in **Figure 14.3**.

Figure 14.3
Activating Fraud Management filters in a Website Payments Pro account.

3. Check the filters you want to use. (The first time you do this, you will be asked to agree to the Terms of Service for Fraud Management filters.)

4. For each filter chosen, click the drop-down options list and select an action for that filter.

5. When a filter should be triggered by an associated value, enter that amount into the Value field.

6. Click Save. Your payment filter options will be configured.

Reporting Fraud

So…do you think someone just tried to pull a fast one on you? It's important for businesses to report any suspected instances of fraud to PayPal, no matter how small. Not only does this protect you, but it also helps to protect other PayPal customers who might fall victim to possible fraud.

Reporting Unauthorized Activity on Your PayPal Account

If you notice unauthorized account activity, this could mean that someone has hacked into your PayPal account. You should report this immediately to the Resolution Center.

PayPal INSIDER

Phishing Emails and Websites

If you receive a questionable email purporting to be from PayPal, or if you're directed to an official-looking PayPal website that doesn't have the proper www.paypal.com address, chances are there's a phishing scam trying to reel you in. Not only should you *not* click any links within the email or on the website, but you should also report the issue to PayPal. The best way to do this is to forward the fake email to spoof@paypal.com. Likewise, you can send an email to spoof@paypal.com containing the URL of the spoof website.

1. From the My Account tab, click the Resolution Center link. The Resolution Center page will open.

2. Click the Dispute a Transaction button. The Report a Problem page will open.

3. Select the Unauthorized Transaction option and click the Continue button. Follow the onscreen instructions to report the issue.

Reporting Unauthorized Activity on Your PayPal Debit Card

If you have a PayPal debit card and notice unauthorized transactions, you should immediately call the number listed on the back of the card. Alternatively, you can email PayPal at the address listed on the back of the card. In either case, be prepared to provide details about the transactions in question.

NOTE: All emails from PayPal will address you by first and last name, so if it says "Dear PayPal Member," it's probably not legitimate.

The Last Word

Social media can bring a lot of opportunities to your business, but it can also invite people in who are trying to separate you from your hard-earned gains. But if you stay alert, use the tools you have available, and above all else, take your time if the alarm bells are going off in your head, you should be able to minimize your chances of being on the wrong end of a fraud scheme.

In Chapter 15, "Using PayPal Tools for Non-Profits," we'll look at the various tools your organization can use to fundraise and keep revenue flowing.

15

Using PayPal Tools for Non-Profits

Raising money to support your non-profit organization's goals and infrastructure is hard work. A lot of effort goes into conveying your mission accurately and how you plan to go about accomplishing that mission, finding people who will support your cause, and then actually accepting the donations themselves.

In this day of electronic payments and instant transactions, you wouldn't think that making it easy for donors to give to your cause would be that difficult, but alas, this is still a challenge for many charitable organizations. Specific rules and customer needs can make fundraising very challenging. Fortunately, there are solutions in place for non-profits.

The Problem: How to Make It Easy?

Collecting funds for any non-profit organization is not always easy. Charitable campaigns need to be carefully planned because there's a lot that's involved in the collection of donations.

The use of social media by a non-profit organization can capitalize on the fact that the friends, relatives, and co-workers of a cause's existing supporters are the most likely potential donors to that cause. Sharing information about the non-profit from friend to friend, including rich media campaign content such as videos and photos, is a great way to spread the word about a charity and its cause.

Cash, Check, Charge, *and* PayPal

Long gone are the days when you could count on setting out a can near the cash register and collecting funds for your cause. With so many organizations vying for customers' attention at merchant locations, it can be a fight to even get a collection device placed at such a location, let alone count on people actually paying with cash and putting their change in the device.

The fact is, fewer people pay with cash anymore. In 2010, U.S. consumers' use of cash dropped by three percent—a rate of decline that's expected to continue through 2015. It's not a universal trait or a given, mind you. In fact, some studies are seeing an increased use of cash in order to avoid using credit cards and racking up more disposable debt.

How this will end up is anyone's guess, but even if cash is used as a financial medium, there are still inherent problems for non-profits. Handling cash is cumbersome and time-consuming—not to mention that the risk of theft goes up quite a bit. On the plus side, cash is still immediately available for use, and because there's no transaction fee, the non-profit can get the full donation amount.

Cash also brings with it the possibility of loss through miscounting. Even the best counters can trip up when counting all those bills and change, which necessitates (at the very least) double-counting everything or else running the risk of miscounting your funds.

Paper checks are a little better, in that they're harder to steal, and, as with cash, there is no transaction fee for checks, so the non-profit gets the full donation amount. But they can still be lost or miscounted. Handling checks also requires manual processing, trips to the bank, manual reconciliation, dealing with insufficient funds, and bounced check fees, as well as the time to clear funds when the check is good.

Some charities avoid this whole issue by setting up a merchant's account to enable donations by credit card. That's one way to do it, but if you do that, you will have higher development costs on your website and the responsibility to keep everything secure. The logistics alone pretty much preclude smaller non-profits from successfully launching such an effort.

But the ability to accept credit cards from your website is really a necessity for non-profits today. Not having an easy way for donors to give to your cause from your website severely limits your fundraising effectiveness and is a missed opportunity.

PayPal has made it easy with the Donate button. In a short amount of time, a non-profit can open a PayPal account, generate a Donate button, copy and paste it to the website, and start accepting donations online. PayPal does require your non-profit to provide documentation and verify your bank account before you can transfer funds out of your PayPal account, a process that will take a few days if everything is submitted in a timely fashion.

Many non-profits that use PayPal also have reported that they saw an increase in donations when they added PayPal. PayPal has more than 100 million active users with more than $4 billion in stored value in their accounts that is spent and donated every two weeks. In fact, in 2011 PayPal helped more than 200,000 non-profits raise over $2 billion.

Would You Like a Receipt?

While many donors are not always looking for a benefit for themselves, there's no getting around the fact that a lot of donations are made to take advantage of the various federal and state tax breaks afforded those who donate to qualified charitable organizations.

If you run such an organization, then you know that providing official receipts for donors who want to take deductions can be an administrative hassle. Often, it has to be done in batches, after the original donation was made, thus increasing the chances for error.

This problem is highlighted when others are accepting donations on your organization's behalf, and they do not have the ability to provide official receipts.

Bookkeeping Problems

Along with the task of getting the proper receipts out to your donors, you may also have problems with bookkeeping in general. Keeping track of multiple donations coming in from multiple channels, alongside all the operating expenses and other accounting, is a huge undertaking.

Automating the tracking of your donations as they come in would be the ideal way of managing this information, in order to avoid bookkeeping errors.

Lost Payments

Handling cash and checks can also lead to payments that are actually lost, which is a terrible thing to have happen. You've lost revenue that you really don't need to lose, and you may likely have damaged the trust of your donor.

Again, electronic payments are one way to avoid this problem, but smaller organizations may not think they have the luxury of implementing electronic payments.

Muddled Messaging

Another problem with collecting funds is less financial and more social: depending on who is doing the asking, your organization's mission statement, and how it's accomplishing that mission, can get muddled as time goes by.

Even the most well-meaning person may inadvertently mix up the message you are trying to convey for others to help reflect your organization's goals. Even your own staff members could misrepresent the message sometimes, but the problem is particularly endemic in people who are trying to raise money on behalf of your organization.

A unified message to the public is important for any non-profit to succeed.

The Solution: Social Media Donation Acceptance

All these problems are real, and they affect non-profits and charities all the time. For well-established organizations, this is all part of the way business gets done. But what about those people who just want to raise money for something that's important, but not a long-term cause?

These types of causes must often resort to face-to-face fundraising, pulling together donations by going door-to-door or asking friends and family. Many people will think that the difficulty is all part of the process...but what if it could be easier?

Accept Donations with FundRazr

ConnectionPoint Systems is a company that has tapped directly into the security and processing power of PayPal to create an online tool for Facebook that lets you raise money for your charitable organization or personal cause.

FundRazr is well integrated into Facebook: it's a full-featured app that can be added to the wall of your Facebook account or that of your organization. You can easily customize the look of your FundRazr with a photo and messaging, and even revise your fundraising goal. Each time you update your FundRazr, the change will appear in your (or your organization's) news feed, reminding your social network of your cause and providing the opportunity for supporters to give easily from their own news feed. If people in your social network feel compelled to join you in the fundraising effort, they can copy and paste your FundRazr to their own wall. All donations that your friends generate from their social network are still directed to your (or your organization's) PayPal account.

Since your supporters use PayPal, their payments are secure, instantaneous, and easily tracked.

FundRazr lets you avoid a lot of fundraising and donation collection headaches, and this simplicity of the collection method makes it easier for donors to give to your cause.

Giving with WhatGives!?

The WhatGives!? app is very similar to the FundRazr app. Like FundRazr, WhatGives!? enables donors to click a single button and give money directly to a cause.

There are some differences, of course. WhatGives!? is not limited to Facebook, for instance. WhatGives!? applications can be placed on Facebook, blogs, and even Web pages.

WhatGives!? also has another great benefit: the capability of being shared. A fundraising organization can have supporters and friends of the organization copy the widget created by the WhatGives!? app and post that widget on their WhatGives!? walls. Not only does this get the collection tool for the charitable cause out there in front of more eyeballs, but all of the money collected goes right back into the organization's central PayPal account, accepting donations for the cause.

Using a centralized account avoids the bookkeeping tangle of donations coming in for an organization that are paid to the supporter, who then has to collect the checks and cash and make sure the money is delivered properly to the main organization. It also gets around the issue of checks made out to the supporter and not the organization, because WhatGives!? sends donations directly to the central organization.

By bringing all of the money through multiple collection points into a central account and being flexible about where it can be posted, WhatGives!? is a great app for non-profits to use.

Support Your Candidate with BigCanvass

In the U.S., political campaigns cost money. A lot of money. Signs, buttons, newspaper, radio, and TV ads—all these can rack up some serious costs.

Raising money for campaigns is hard, thankless work sometimes. There are very strict campaign fundraising rules to which candidates must adhere, and there's a limit on individual donations. So campaigns must try to get large donations from corporate donors (which is not often politically expedient), and try to get a lot of smaller donations in a grassroots effort (which can be slower).

BigCanvass is a social giving app that can help. Built by the same people who created WhatGives!?, BigCanvass supports all of the same features of that app, including allowing users to post on Facebook and blogs, as well as copying the widget onto their Web pages.

BigCanvass adds more features specifically for campaigns, most notably detailed reports that many campaigns must have in order to comply with local and federal election laws. Contributor information is also a prime source for more supporter information down the road.

Electioneering is an expensive process, and BigCanvass is a handy tool to help mitigate those costs and enable grassroots support.

Using FundRazr

In order to give you an idea of just how easy it is to use these products, here are the steps involved in linking to, installing, and using FundRazr in your Facebook account. Before beginning, you must make sure that you already have a vetted non-profit PayPal account.

1. In your Facebook account, enter FundRazr in the Search field. The FundRazr app will appear in the list of results.

2. Click on the FundRazr app option. The FundRazr page will appear.

3. Click the Get Started Now button. If this is the first time you have used FundRazr, an authorization dialog will appear.

4. Click the Log In and Add to Facebook button. The Create a FundRazr page will appear.

NOTE: If the name of the organization will be shown in your fundraising widget, you will need to select the For an Organization option.

5. Select the option you want to use by clicking its Go button. In this example, we have clicked the organization option, so the Sign up an Organization page will appear.

6. Enter your name and organization information and select the Type of Organization. The Details section of the app will appear.

7. Enter the pertinent information on the organization. In the PayPal account section, enter the email address for the organization's PayPal account and click the Check It! button. If valid, a Valid status message will appear.

8. Complete the remainder of the options on the page and click the Sign Up Now button. The Options page will appear.

9. Many of the options are pre-included in FundRazr, so click the Next button. The Build It! page will appear.

Now that the account setup is complete for your FundRazr app, it's time to configure the actual widget itself.

1. In the Title & Description section, enter the relevant information.

2. Click the Theme section. The Theme palette will appear.

3. Choose a background color. The color will be applied to the widget.

4. Click the Image & Video section. The Image tool will appear.

5. Click the Browse for Image button. The Select File dialog will appear.

6. Select the image to upload and click Open. The image will be uploaded and will appear in the widget.

7. Click the Currency & Goal section. This section will appear.

8. Enter the appropriate currency and goal amount and click the Payment Amounts section. This section will appear.

9. Choose the increment amounts you want to give donors as a payment option. If you want to add additional increments, enter them in the Amount field and click Add.

10. Click the Collect Donor Info section, which will open this final section.

11. Set what information you want to collect.

12. Click Save. The application will appear in the app's home page.

NOTE: When the FundRazr installation is first completed, there is a period of waiting while the organization for which you are raising money is contacted to make sure that you are authorized to collect money on the organization's behalf.

After the FundRazr installation is approved, you can click the Publish to a Page link to have the application appear on your Facebook page. After you set up FundRazr, the social sharing begins with spreading the word on the campaign. In addition to Facebook sharing and messaging, customers can also tweet and send email messages about the fundraising campaign from within FundRazr.

TIP: FundRazr has other functionalities that you can request and add when you want. One handy tool allows you to build campaigns that funnel money directly to the non-profit, so you can track the money without actually having to manage it.

The Last Word

As you can see, setting up an app like FundRazr in Facebook is very easy. WhatGives!? and BigCanvass function in much the same way, affording you a lot of flexibility to connect your social media audience to any fundraising activity you need.

In Chapter 16, "10 Ways to Profit Through Social Media," we'll wrap up the book with a look at the best ways to implement social media for the benefit of your organization.

10 Ways to Profit Through Social Media

Social media, when used correctly, can be a great asset to your organization. Whether your organization is commercial or non-profit, legacy or start-up, the ability to directly connect your organization with supporters can build loyalty and a stronger customer relationship than ever.

As we have emphasized throughout this book, social media, like any other tool, needs to be used properly to maximize its performance. In this chapter, we will review 10 key ways that succcessful organizations apply social media plans for the best results and profit.

1. Set Your Strategy

There are three reasons why you shouldn't start using social media platforms without a plan.

First, your parents' advice about thinking before you speak definitely holds true in social media, because what you say in cyberspace can and will be remembered (and recalled) for a long time.

Thinking before you speak or otherwise engage people on the Internet is also important because it takes a long time to build good relationships but just a few ill-chosen words to damage a relationship irreparably. This is reason number one why you should have a strategy in place for social media.

Second, you need to know what your overall message will be. This is just business common sense—if you have a marketing and advertisement strategy in place already, you don't want to throw a wrench into it and start delivering another message entirely. The strongest message is the most coordinated message.

Third, it's very important to recognize that like most technology, tools will change, and often very quickly. Many social media networks could be obsolete in a year's time, or less. That's the nature of technology.

This is why it's critical to craft a plan that delivers a message or set of messages that you want to convey and then push those messages out on the platforms where your customers are. If that platform happens to be only Twitter, then fine. But you need to open the conversation to your customers on whatever sites they are using.

2. Research Your Audience

It's the age-old problem for business owners: in order to sell to customers, you have to first find customers. In pre-electronic times, it was simpler: hang a sign out on a storefront, and if your products and services were good and your prices fair, then the customers would come through the door.

Today, it's harder. With more competition and customers spread out all over town, or even the world, it's harder than ever to find people with whom to do business. But not impossible.

First, leverage the knowledge of people and organizations that have been in your shoes. They're the experienced ones, the thought leaders and knowledge managers of your particular interest or business sector.

Also, seek out people who will have a direct connection to or interest in your efforts.

Just asking your customers what social media platforms they use should be the first mode of discovery. A lot of business owners assume that there's some special trick to figuring out where their customers reside online. And while there are some ways to find this information on your own, you can do the easy task first and simply ask.

Be proactive, too; it's important to advertise that you are on the Internet, ready to be followed.

Use the social media platform's own tools to find out who's on that platform. All you usually need are the email addresses of your customers to conduct such a search.

3. Join Conversations

At first, you might be tempted to simply broadcast all that you think is great about your organization—its product, its people, its brand—all the qualities you love about your company. That's a common place to start, but understand that if you keep doing that, the novelty will wear off quickly.

Remember, this is always a conversation, no matter what type of social media platform you're working with. That means it can't be a one-way broadcast of just the aspects of your business you find interesting. Be prepared to engage your audience, just as you would if they were customers in your store.

When you do this, you will tap into the main value of social media: you're holding a conversation with someone, but everyone else can listen in.

If the conversation ends well, people will look at this and think that you must have a business that's interested in the needs of its customers.

Meanwhile, offer compelling points of interest so that people will want to converse with you. This might be content on your blog or other social outlet, but it won't be a broadcast because that would be counter-productive. You will need to strike a balance between talking and listening, with the understanding that people will mostly want to learn from and listen to you but will expect to be heard when they do have something to tell you.

4. Find the Right Tools

A big reason we haven't seen a lot of business tools integrated into social media platforms yet is because it's not easy implementing a transaction system that is safe and secure within an environment that was not designed for ecommerce. Social networks are great for conversations, but not so great (yet) at ecommerce.

This is about to change. There are tools that that will create a tighter integration between social conversation and commerce online. Many major corporations are working to make social commerce happen very soon.

Social media platforms are all about open information distribution. This is problematic when it comes to your financial information. "Open" and "financial data" aren't two terms that mix particularly well. PayPal plans to be right at that intersection by being a layer of protection for your financial information online, regardless of the medium for the transaction—traditional Web ecommerce sites or social media platforms.

Beyond social commerce tools, apply the right tools for your social media content management. There are a great many tools to manage multiple social media accounts on more than one social media platform. HootSuite and TweetDeck are good examples of tools in this category.

5. Create Relevant Content

One great way to figure out the most relevant content is to determine what your visitors want when they come to your company ecommerce site, blog, or social media site.

As users look for information that's relevant to them and your organization, they will plug search terms into their favorite search engine and find the content they seek. If your content is a match, your site will be prominently displayed in the search results.

These organic searches will help you figure out what content is most interesting to your visitors, and what will likely be interesting to them in the future. This is search engine optimization 101: tailoring your content to attract the attention of the audience and customers you want. Using these kinds of SEO analytics can be of great assistance in creating your social media conversations.

Listen to other conversations in your topic area of interest, too. Knowing what others are interested in will give you a pretty clear picture of how to jump in on the conversation.

6. Use Rich Media

Producing content of great interest to others is all well and good.

But what if you could go further, and actually encourage users to contribute new and original content of their own?

This is what is known as *organic content:* content contributed by users is not only a feature of social media sites but is also a prerequisite.

There are several ways to encourage users to contribute content to your social media channels. One manner is through rich multimedia content, which has become very easy to produce these days, and is an effective way to get participation. Use polls, images, and video to get your audience involved in the conversation.

7. Listen to Customers

Once you locate these conversations, see what they're saying. What's the hot topic right now? Is it directly related to a product or service you provide? How is the tone of the discussion?

These are concepts that you will need to note as you listen to the conversation. Hold off on responding for a bit; wait a few days to get the gist of the discussion.

For instance, are your peers in the conversation? What are they saying? You don't necessarily want to parrot them, because you'll sound like someone who's just a "me too" sort of chatterer. Listen to what's being said and by whom. You may find yourself agreeing or disagreeing with a lot of ideas, so you'll want to take the time to figure out what you're going to say and to whom.

Another use of social media channels is to utilize them as a direct customer service conduit to your customers. If you are a smaller company, this is an ideal way for customers to get their questions asked and answered.

That's because even though phone calls and email still work, many customers find it more satisfying to complain in a fully public forum, where not only the company will hear their complaints but other people will as well. This gives the customer a sense of accountability from the organization, and any organization that ignores such questions and comments would be foolish.

As part of your work in social media, you must be ready to monitor social media for such questions, and then answer them as promptly and completely as possible. This is not to say you have to drop everything to get to them, but it wouldn't be a bad idea to check in during lulls in your day. If you have a dedicated customer service team already, you should definitely assign resources to monitor social media channels and respond to questions.

8. Build Community

The common error in community building is putting the organization's welfare before the community's welfare.

When building a community with social media, you must put the community first and and enjoy your business payoff later. An online community can help foster brand loyalty, build self-driven customer support groups, and even help create a better product—all benefits that can greatly improve your bottom line.

A sincere effort must be applied to the community you're trying to create, because community members can spot blatant marketing a mile off, and when they do, they will assuredly leave you alone.

When you start any community, you must define goals for community members. They need to be able to do something, because no matter how much they love the product, they will not participate in the community for long if nothing draws their participation.

9. Collaborate with Your Audience

Social media can also encourage collaborative efforts that can benefit your organization.

Your customers might know a lot about things you know nothing about. Working together, then, can help you tap into their expertise, and can also enable them to tap into yours. The outcome of such collaboration is to create something that is better than what you could do separately.

Your clientele are very smart about what they want and need…you just have to tap into their ideas and find out.

10. Measure Your Results

There are quite a few social media metrics that you can begin tracking right away. Some of the most effective analytics derive directly from Web media as the findings show how social media drives traffic to your website, where users may become buyers on your ecommerce site.

Social Media SUCCESS STORY

C'est Cheese: Getting Results

Mari feels her social media efforts have been successful, but that's a gut feeling not based on any hard numbers. Now, a few months into her efforts, she finally has the time to sit down and analyze what's been happening.

As she conducted her various social media activities, Mari kept track of how many hours she and her employees spent on social media. With that figure, she can calculate the amount of time (and money) C'est Cheese has invested in social media.

Measuring the metrics on the store's blog, she sees that her monthly traffic has increased by about 8 percent. This is good, but Mari was aiming for 10 percent, so she resolves to spend more time generating content on the blog. Recipe blog posts are still the most popular, so she thinks she can reach out to local restaurants for more inspiration and get some cross-promotional activity.

The number of her followers on Facebook and Twitter has grown and she is pleased with the interactivity on those platforms, as Mari and her staff have not had to spend a lot of time answering queries directly from customers and followers, since many of the topics are frequently addressed by others.

It's been a little harder to track how many of those conversations have led to actual sales. In-store and website sales are up, so Mari has a feeling the social media is helping, but she hasn't tracked sales well enough to understand if these additional sales are coming from the social media interactions. She further resolves to track sales better to get a more complete picture of her social media success.

In all, Mari's analysis is positive: the amount of time spent on social media is about 20 hours per week for Mari and her staff, and the uptick in sales has more than covered the cost of their time.

Like a good cheese, a successful social media plan takes some time to age properly. So far, C'est Cheese's social media strategy is doing well, and Mari knows where to focus her efforts next.

After she samples that new shipment of Manchego cheese that just came in.

Even if you don't sell products and services on the Web, you can still use these metrics, because you can track in-bound traffic to your business by monitoring how many people send you emails based on your social activity, or fill out the "contact us" form on your website.

These metrics include user leads, page bounces, network size, and online mentions. Blogs fall into a unique position within social media metrics because they are social media platforms in and of themselves, as well as great generators of social media conversations.

That is a lot of social media data that you can gather for your business, but gathering data alone is not enough. You have to apply that data to measuring the achievement of specific goals.

Measuring the true impact of your social media activity is not going to be a simple matter of tracking one or two statistics and then calling it done. You will need to compile different sets of data and use them in combination to determine the intent of your audience and how you can enhance the conversation as well as achieve your business goals.

The (Very) Last Word

We hope we've sparked some new ideas about how you can integrate social media within your organization's overall strategy, as well as combine the tools of PayPal with social media tactics to get a direct benefit for your organization.

The social commerce field is only going to grow as time goes by, as more and more companies innovate new ways to connect ecommerce to social media users. Stay on top of this growing field of technology and business, because someday (probably soon), it will become part of your business plan and your success.

Index